THE ESSENTIAL GUIDE
TO EVERYTHING HAMPTONS

By
TRACEY HOLMES

DEDICATION
To my amazing family.

Table of Contents

Hello from the author...

I'm so excited to introduce the second edition of The Hamptons Lifesaver.

My book came about by happenstance. In 2017 the fabulous restaurant - EMP Summer House - came to East Hampton as a seasonal pop-up while their extremely successful NYC restaurant Eleven Madison Park was being renovated. Lucky for me, they brought their entire crew from the city with them. It occurred to me that the majority of them had probably never spent much time in the Hamptons. Being their realtor, I found myself putting together lists of services and things to do on their days off. Before I knew it, that list had grown into a mini guide book. Staples print center saw quite a bit of me during those couple of weeks before it grew into an actual book. Once the book started to sell, I realized that there's been a hole in the guide book industry for the Hamptons for almost 10 years. With the influx of tourists and new homeowners each year, paired with the ever-changing village scenery, we were definitely long overdue!

My 2018 edition has grown to include an array of new services, galleries, resources for pets, and more. Every summer brings new experiences, so I hope I didn't forget anything!

There's so much to explore on the eastern end of Long Island on both the North and South Forks. I hope you use this book as a guide to discover each of our charming, historical villages; the uniqueness of the area and why people have been coming back year after year for over 100 years.

Enjoy your stay.

See you at the beach. Or at the dog park!

Cheers,

Tracey

A drive through a *Little* History...

The Hamptons are so deeply embedded with history it would be a shame to leave it out of my 2018 edition. This is especially true for those who have never visited our little part of heaven. I'm crazy about history but I understand many are not! We are more than just beautiful white sandy beaches, spectacular farmland vistas, fabulous restaurants and shopping. Believe it or not, the Hamptons are rich with American history and many notable past events.

I've summered the majority of my life in Southampton. I consider it my home. Our family summer house has a long historical background. The gorgeous Georgian Manor House was built in 1913 for Charles Blair MacDonald who named it Ballysheer. MacDonald was the grandfather of American golf. He built the first 18-hole golf course in America. His courses include our Hamptons own National Golf Links of America. This linkage to history was instrumental in feeding my appetite for local lore and all it entailed.

The South Fork of Long Island was settled by colonist from Massachusetts in the seventeenth century and for almost 300 years consisted primarily of farming communities. Known as potato farm country, the Hamptons changed to a destination summer resort spot for the wealthy in the late nineteenth century.

Let's go on a historical driving tour. Buckle up and enjoy the ride. We'll start in Southampton because it truly is the beginning. After crossing over the Shinnecock Canal, traveling west to east, our first stop is the Village of Southampton.

Southampton is the oldest and the largest of the Townships. It is New York state's oldest English colony. The 10 original settlers landed on Conscience Point from Lynn Massachusetts in 1640. Eight square miles of land was granted to the colonist by James Ferrill, an agent of Lord Sterling of England. At the time the land was occupied by the Shinnecock Indian Tribe and the deeded trade between them was said to include 16 coats and 3 score bushels of corn (approximately 210 lbs. of corn by today's' standards). Between 1640 - 1643 the population had increased to 43 families. By the mid-18th century the colony had grown to encompass nearly 300 square miles, however over half of that land was and still is to this day, underwater.

Leaving Southampton and continuing to travel east on Montauk Highway (our 2-lane highway), the next stop is Water Mill. In 1644 England granted Edward Howell, a Puritan from Buckinghamshire England, 40 acres upon which to build a mill. Howell was one of the original 10 settlers and his mill served the local farms as a place to grind their grain into meal. Unnamed settlements that popped up at that time were referred to as "east" or "west" of the water mills. By the 1800's it became known as Water Mills and later Water Mill.

You can't drive through Water Mill without noticing the enormous waterfront house on your right known as Villa Maria. It was built in 1897 as the summer home for 2 cousins who were Industrial Financiers. Needing to dress up the front lawn the cousins purchased a windmill in North Haven and had it hauled to the Village Green, where it still stands today! The estate passed through three owners before being sold to The Sisters of Saint Dominic in 1931. It remained in the hands of the nuns until 2005 when it was sold as a private residence. It's rumored that President Theodore Roosevelt's favorite horse General Ruxton is buried somewhere on the grounds.

Our next stop is Bridgehampton, originally named Bullhead. Its settlers started the community at the head of Sagg Pond. In 1686 a bridge was built connecting Mecox with Sagaponack which caused the towns' name to change from Bullhead to Bridgehampton. It was the slowest to develop when compared to its neighboring establishments of Sag Harbor and East Hampton. Each of them were bustling villages with neatly planned streets, homes and establishments. Bridgehampton was a farming community mostly involved in both agriculture and trade. Thanks to the farmlands that existed for hundreds of years before, Bridgehampton now boasts the largest commercial shopping space in the Hamptons - Bridgehampton Commons.

Veering off Montauk highway in Bridgehampton and heading North on Bridge-Sag Turnpike you'll hit the old whaling village of Sag Harbor. It's not entirely clear when Sag Harbor came into existence but was somewhere between 1701-1730. Its name was derived from a tuber (a nutty version of the potato) grown by the Metoac Algonquins. The Metoac name for the tuber was sagabon - hence Sag Harbor became both the village and the harbor name. Sag Harbor developed into a major international port for the whaling industry producing whale oil. In 1797 George Washington declared it a major whaling center. By 1798 it had more commercial ships in its harbor than New York City and was made the first official port upon entering the United States. With the vast amount of ships entering port, the first customs house on Long Island was built in town. The village fell into a state of decline in the mid-19th century when the whaling trade dried up due to the emerging petroleum industry. It was also hit by three major fires in the 1800's, that engulfed the village, leaving it in a state of disrepair. However, by 1869 the LIRR was running to Sag Harbor bringing in tourism and the town began to flourish once again. Until 1895 this train line was the furthest east the RR ran. In 1939 the line was shut down entirely.

Wealthy residents of Sag Harbor began building stately homes that rivalled its neighboring village of Southampton. If you drive through the streets immediately after leaving the village you will see beautiful Federal style homes from the booming whale industry days. By the 19th century Gothic and Greek Revival, Italianate and Georgian residences began springing up as summer estates. Some of these are now museums such as The Sag Harbor Whaling and Historical Museum on Main Street. Many continue to be privately occupied.

Continue driving east on Route 114 and East Hampton is the

next village you'll hit. East Hampton is a peninsula (The South Fork) surrounded by the Atlantic Ocean on the south side and Gardiners, Fort Pond and Napeague bays on the North side. It was founded in 1648 primarily for farming, fishing and whaling by Presbyterian farmers. At that time, it was a 31,000-acre parcel that was a portion of a larger parcel of a land trade made between Chief Wyandanch of the Montaukett tribe and the state of Connecticut (at that time NY had yet to be declared a state). Once it was, it became the first English settlement in the state of New York. Its original name was Maidstone. However, following suit with the other "Hamptons" such as Southampton and Westhampton, in 1664 the name was changed to East Hampton. East Hampton was slower to develop than Southampton. The original houses were small village clapboard houses built for fishermen and farmers. It was a full 20 years behind its sister village Southampton. Until 1895, the rail line ended in Bridgehampton. When the line finally extended to East Hampton and Montauk, an east end real estate boom began. Although on a more modest housing scale when compared to the shingled mega mansions being built in Southampton at that time.

By the 1800's East Hampton was invoking inspiration for artists. Plein-Air art colonies in East Hampton and the Shinnecock Summer School of Art in Southampton began to attract artists to the area and remains a large art community of well-known artists owning homes and studios. The artistic inspiration continues. Take a visit to the Jackson-Pollack museum on Springs Fireplace Road. It's where he lived and worked, and it feels like he just ran out for a smoke. It's that unchanged.

Just a 3-mile hop down Montauk Highway we come to the tiny hamlet of Amagansett. With less than 1,500 residents and occupying only 6 square miles, it has been a popular beach resort and home to many celebrities for years. In 1942, four unwelcomed visitors were dropped at Atlantic beach from a German U-boat. They were spies whose intention was to infiltrate and sabotage American industry. They made their way to the railroad leaving out of Amagansett and headed to NYC. One spy turned coat to the FBI, the plot was blown, and they were foiled. They were tried for war crimes and put to death.

At the end of the last ice-age Amagansett was the easternmost tip of Long Island. After several thousand years of ever changing ocean currents the sand filled a stretch of land (now called the Napeague stretch) joining Amagansett and an island in the Atlantic now known as Montauk. This brings our driving journey to "The End". Montauk is a tourist hotspot with six state parks, beautiful ocean vistas and more saltwater fishing records than any port in the world. It has a laid-back beach feeling that is more prominent than in any other village in the Hamptons. In the 1600's, a large land exchange took place with the Montaukett tribe who resided on the land that is now the Hamptons. This particular parcel ran from Southampton to the bluffs of Hither Hills state park. Later, in 1660, the widow of Chief Wyandanch traded the remaining tribal land running from Hither Hills to the Point of Montauk for 100£ to be paid in corn and wampum. The land has seen so many uses over the years. In the 1600's it was rich grazing land for cattle and sheep. In 1792 George Washington commissioned the first lighthouse in the state of NY on Montauk Point. In the 1898's Roosevelts Rough Riders set up a temporary camp for over 20,000 soldiers who were being quarantined for malaria after fighting the Spanish in Cuba. Called Camp Wykoff, it comprised of 5000 acres. It has been divided into 3 of the state parks in Montauk.

In the 1920's Carl Fisher had plans to turn it into a Miami Beach like get away. He built the Montauk Manor, the tall building in the center of town for offices, the golf course and the yacht club. His vision ended with the crash of 1929. In the 1940's a coastal defense station was commissioned by the US army and was disguised as a fishing village to ward off enemy ships. It is now Camp Hero. So much of the history has been preserved in Museums and parks that are open to the public. Pack a picnic or grab a bite and take a walking tour of the cliffs. There are tons of walking trails. It's truly spectacular. If you want to see a sunset to knock your socks off, stay the whole day. You won't regret it.

Nestled between the North and South forks is our half- sister,

Shelter Island. Many may not consider it an actual "Hampton", however it has grown into a desirable destination. It's quiet and has so many interesting historical houses and fantastic restaurants it would be a shame to leave this non-Hampton out. Reachable only by ferry, this island is more than half water and marshland. One third of the island is currently owned by the Nature Conservancy and is a protected wildlife preserve with four nature and bird watching trails. Originally occupied by the Manhanset tribe, their name for it translated to "island sheltered by islands". Trading hands multiple times by 1651 the then owner Stephen Goodyear sold it to a group of Barbados sugar merchants for 1,600 pounds of sugar. One of those sugar merchants became the islands first settler and in 1652 he built the first house for his 17-year-old bride. The island was used for farming and multiple plots were sold. Subsequently split up by marriages, by the early 18th century 20 families resided on the island. Shelter Island Heights was developed in 1871 as a summer resort to hold camp meetings. During the eight years the meetings were being held on the island, 70 cottages were built in the classic American style. This area is now a National Historical area. On the south side of the island tycoons such as Francis Smith, the Borax King, and Artemas Ward, the mass marketing wizard built huge summer homes that are still standing today. There are many residents living on Shelter with roots that date back to the Americana Revolution. Some summer residents are fifth generation homeowners.

If you can, take a boat ride around the entire island and look at the expansive estates and the beautiful scenery. Or, rent a bike and tour the island stopping off at one of the many restaurants in Chapter 15 along the way. End the day at Sunset Beach. If you're on a boat, call a water taxi to take you to shore. Or you can swim! Once there, you must try the frozen Rose at the Sunset Beach bar. It's delish. Then sit back, listen to the music and enjoy watching the spectacular sun going down. It's quite a way to end your day.

I hope to decide to embark on my little driving tour while you're visiting the east end. You'll be happy you did!

ALL THE BASICS

CHAMBERS OF COMMERCE

East Hampton
58B Park Place
631-324-0362
www.easthamptonchamber.com

Montauk
742 Montauk Hwy
631-668-2428
www.montaukchamber.com

Sag Harbor
55 Main Street
631-725-0011
www.sagharborchamber.com

Southampton
76 S. Main Street
631-283-0402
www.southamptonchamber.com

DRY CLEANERS
Bridgehampton

King Kullen-Dutch Girl Cleaners & Shoe Repair
2044 Montauk Highway - Bridgehampton Commons
631-537-5138

East Hampton

East Hampton Cleaners
104 Newtown Lane
631-324-0036

North Main Street Cleaners
120 N Main Street
631-324-1640

Southampton

Hampton Arrow Cleaners
84 Main St.
631-283-0059

Southampton Village Dry Cleaners
56 Jagger Ln
631-238-2299
*sewing and alteration

Wainscott

Sweet Waters French Style Dry Cleaners
350 Montauk Highway
631-537-5120

Water Mill

Water Mill Cleaners
1760 Montauk Highway
631-726-6400

EMERGENCY
FIRE DEPARTMENTS

Amagansett Fire Department
631-267-3300

Bridgehampton Fire Department
631-324-4477

East Hampton Fire Department
631-324-0124

Montauk Fire Department
631-668-5695

North Sea Fire Department
631-283-4739

Sag Harbor Fire Department
631-725-0252
631-324-0124

Shelter Island Fire Department
631-749-0184

Southampton Village Fire Department
631-283-0072

Wainscott Fire Department
631-296-8066

POLICE

East Hampton Police
631-537-7575

Montauk Police Precinct
631-668-3709

Sag Harbor Village Police
.631-725-0058

Shelter Island Police Department
631-749-0600

Southampton Town Police
631-728-3400

Southampton Village Police Department
631-283-0056

Wainscott Police Department
631-537-7575

MEDICAL

East Hampton Urgent Care Center
470 Montauk Hwy – East Hampton
631-329-5900
7 days a week   9:00 a.m.-5:00 p.m.
www.easthamptonurgentcare.com

Sag Harbor Walk in Medical Clinic
Dr. Ilona Polak MD
34 Bay Street, Sag Harbor
631-808-3337
Mon-Fri   9:00 a.m. – 5:00 p.m.
Sat   9:30 a.m. – 1:00 p.m.
www.sagharborwalkin.com

Southampton Hospital and Emergency Room
240 Meeting House Lane - Southampton
7 days/24 hours
631-726-8200

Southampton Urgent Medical Care
Dr. Mark Kot MD
609 Hampton Rd - Southampton
631-204-9600
Mon-Fri   8:00 a.m. – 5:00 p.m.
Saturday   8:00 a.m. – 4:00 p.m.
Sunday   8:00 a.m. – 3:00 p.m.
www.southamptonurgentmedicalcare.com

Wainscott Walk in Medical Clinic
83 Wainscott Northwest Road - East Hampton
631-537-1892
Mon-Fri   8:30 a.m. – 4:00 p.m.
Sat   8:30 a.m. – 1:00 p.m

4

EXTERMINATORS

East End Pest Control
10 Smith Street – Shelter Island
631-749-8952
www.eastendpestcontrol.com

East End Tick & Mosquito Control
214 N. Sea Road – Southampton
631-287-9700 – SH
631-324-9700 - EH

Hampton Pest Management
22 Old Country Road – Quogue
631-324-1333
www.hamptonpestmanagement.com

Jim's Busy Bee Pest Control
152 Montauk Hwy – Southampton
631-283-1016

Nardy's Pest Control
535 County Road 39A – Southampton
631-324-7474
www.nardypest.com

Peconic Pest Control
394 Main Street – Sag Harbor
631-287-7378

Premier Pest Control
1738 County Road 39A – Southampton
631-387-5551
www.premier-pestcontrol.com

Stings N Things
79 Moses Lane - Southampton
631-283-9519
www.stingsnthings.com

Target Pest Control
115 Pantigo Road – East Hampton
631-324-0122

FUEL OIL

Dippel Fuel Oil Inc.
2141 Montauk Hwy – Bridgehampton
631-537-0193

East Hampton Fuel Oil Corp
14 Washington Ave – East Hampton
631-324-2420

Heras Fuel Oil Corp
64 Clinton Street – East Hampton
631-329-0014

Houcks Fuel Oil Company Inc.
333 Riverhead Road – Westhampton
631-288-6600
www.houcksfuel.com

Indigo Fuel
62 Grant Drive – Montauk
631-668-7800
www.indigofuelltd.com

Quogue Sinclair Fuel Inc.
161 W. Montauk Hwy – Hampton Bays
631-728-1066

Royal Petroleum
23 Three Mile Harbor Road – East Hampton
631-658-9100

Schenck Fuels
62 Newtown Lane - East Hampton
631-324-0142
www.schenckfuels.com

Steve's East End Fuel
East Hampton
631-329-9344

Strong Oil Company
938 Montauk Hwy – Water Mill
631-726-0303

Southampton Oil Inc.
1654 County Road 39 – Southampton
631-324-0815

WCESP Inc.
2141 Main Street – Bridgehampton
631-537-0193

Slomins
125 Laumin Lane – Hicksville
800-252-7663

GARBAGE SERVICES

Pick Up Services

East End Sanitation
2 Commercial Park Rd - Quogue
631-898-6128

Go Green Sanitation
1691 County Road 39 – Southampton
631-287-8608

Micky's Carting Corp.
34 S. Erie Ave - Montauk
631-668-9120

Norsic & Son
1625 County Road 39 - Southampton
631-283-0604

S&P Sanitation
1062 Montauk Hwy - Watermill
631-726-9500

Suburban Sanitation
92 Clay Pit Road – Sag Harbor
631-725-1347

Sunrise Sanitation
14 Brook Road – Westhampton
631-288-3300

Three R's Residential Carting
9 Fresno Place – East Hampton
631-324-0135

Winters Brothers
211 Springs Fireplace Road - East Hampton
631-324-9656

Dump It Yourself

East Hampton Recycling Center
260 Springs Fireplace Road - East Hampton
631-324-2199
Open: Closed on Wednesday
Yearly Sticker: $115

Montauk Recycling Center
Montauk Highway - Montauk
631-668-5813
Open: Closed on Wednesday
Yearly Sticker: $115

Sag Harbor Transfer Station
485 Main Street – Sag Harbor
631-725-3097
Open: 7 days a week except holidays
Yearly Sticker: Free to residents

Southampton Recycling Center
1370 Majors Path - Southampton
631-283-5210
Open: 7 days a week except holidays
Yearly Sticker: Free to residents. You must use green bag recycling only

HARDWARE STORES

Amagansett

Amagansett Hardware
151 Main Street
631-267-3536

Bridgehampton

Thayer's Hardware & Patio
2434 Montauk Hwy
631-537-0077

East Hampton

Riverhead Building Supply
2 Railroad Avenue
631-324-0300

Village Hardware
32 Newtown Lane
631-324-2456

Montauk

Montauk Hardware
Montauk Highway
631-668-2456

Revco Electrical Supply
94 Industrial Road
631-668-6800

Sag Harbor

Emporium True Value Hardware
72 Main Street
631-725-0103

Henry Persan & Sons
79 Division Street
631-725-1900

Shelter Island

Shelter Island Ace Hardware
4 Grand Avenue
631-749-0097

Southampton

Herrick Hardware
41 Main Street
631-283-0026

Revco Electrical Supply
360 County Road 39A
631-283-3600

Riverhead Building Supply
40 Powell Avenue
631-283-2000

Shinnecock True Value Hardware
849 County Road 39
631-283-2047

Water Mill

Water Mill Building Supply
1110 Montauk Hwy
631-726-4493

Wainscott

Wainscott Hardware
338 Montauk Hwy
631-237-1766

HEAT & AIR SERVICE

East End Heating and Air
631-903-4437
www.eastendheatingandair@yahoo.com

Grant Heating and Cooling
48 Route 114 – East Hampton
631-324-0679
www.suffolkcountyhvac.org

Hardy Heat & Air
76 Mariner Drive – Southampton
631-287-1674
www.hardyhvac.com

Harry Kozen Heating & Air
200 Daniels Hole Road – Wainscott
631-537-1717

Mance Heating and Air Conditioning
44 Three Mile Harbor Road – East Hampton
631-324-5518

Matz/Rightway Heating & Air-conditioning Service
219 W. Montauk Hwy – Hampton Bays
631-728-5405
www.matz-rightway.com

Weber & Grahn Air Conditioning & Heating
216 E. Montauk Hwy – Hampton Bays
631-728-1166
www.weberandgrahn.com

LAUNDROMATS

East Hampton Laundry
497 Montauk Highway - Amagansett
631-267-7725

Montauk Laundromat
5 Elmswood Ave - Montauk
631-668-4349

Sag Harbor Laundrette
20 Main Street - Sag Harbor
631-725-5830

Southampton Village Laundrette
34 Nugent Street - Southampton
631-283-9708

LIBRARIES

Amagansett Free Library
215 Main Street - Amagansett
631-267-3810

East Hampton Library
159 Main Street - East Hampton
631-324-0222

The Hamptons Library of Bridgehampton
Main Street - Bridgehampton
631-537-0015

John Jermain Memorial Library
201 Main Street - Sag Harbor
631-725-0049

Montauk Library - Montauk
871 Montauk Highway - Montauk
631-668-3377

Rogers Memorial Library
91 Coopers Farm Road - Southampton
631-283-0774

Springs Library
Springs Fireplace Road. - East Hampton
631-324-9686

LOCKSMITHS

A1 Locksmith
622 Montauk Hwy - Amagansett
631-318-3070

All Hamptons Locksmith
Southampton
631-276-2456
www.locksmithhamptonsny.com

Bob Bennett Locksmith
East Hampton
631-267-3316

Country Locksmiths
500 N. Main Street – Southampton
631-287-3227

East End Lock
493 County Rd 39 – Southampton
631-283-0763

Johns Lock Service
373 Bridgehampton/Sag Harbor Tpke - Bridgehampton
631-725-4738

Stears Locksmith Service
99 Sag Harbor Tpke – East Hampton
631-725-3273
www.stearslocksmith.com

The Village
4 Hartley Blvd – East Hampton
631-324-2547
www.thevillagelocksmiths.com

PLUMBERS

East Hampton

Brass Plumbing & Heating
631-324-4974

Dicks Plumbing & Heating
631-324-4451

Grand Plumbing & Heating
631-324-5800

Hardy Plumbing Heating & Air Conditioning
631-329-1333

David King Plumbing & Heating
631-324-5718

M&J Radziewicz Plumbing & Heating
631-725-0015

Siedlarz Plumbing
631-324-3500

Montauk

Marco Plumbing & Heating
631-668-9319

Montauk Plumbing & Heating
631-668-8499

Pipemasters Plumbing & Heating
631-668-2122

Prado Brothers Plumbing & Heating
631-668-9169

John B Ward Jr. Plumbing & Heating
631-668-4399

Sag Harbor

Fleming Kevin Plumbing & Heating
631-725-1656

Harbor Plumbing & Heating
631-725-3394

Schiovoni Fuel Oil Heating & Plumbing
631-725-0466

Sean Beal Plumbing
631-725-8588

RM Steffens Plumbing & Heating Inc.
631-725-0002

Shelter Island

Hardy Plumbing & Heating
631-283-1333

Roto-Rooter Plumbing & Drain
631-874-3070

Southampton

Hampton Plumbing
631-283-7070

Hardy Plumbing
631-283-9333
www.hardyplumbing.com

JS Plumbing & Heating
631-283-7175

Kevin Harrington Plumbing & Heating
631-283-8103

North Sea Plumbing & Heating Company
631-283-3876
www.northseaplumbing .com

Okey Plumbing & Heating
631-725-2985
www.okeyplumbing.com

POST OFFICES

AMAGANSETT - 11930
501 Montauk Highway

BRIDGEHAMPTON - 11932
2322 Main Street

EAST HAMPTON - 11937
12 Gay Lane

MONTAUK - 11954
73 South Euclid Avenue

SAG HARBOR - 11963
12 Long Island Avenue

SAGAPONACK - 11962
542 Sagg Main Street

SOUTHAMPTON - 11968
39 Nugent Street

WAINSCOTT - 11975
357 Montauk Highway

WATER MILL - 11976
670 Montauk Highway

PROFESSIONAL SERVICES & OFFICE SUPPLIES

Bridgehampton

Iron Horse Graphics
36 Maple Lane
631-537-3400
www.ironhorsegraphics.com

Staples
2044 Montauk Hwy – Bridgehampton Commons Bridgehampton
631-537-1654
www.staples.com

East Hampton

East Hampton Business Center
20 Park Place
631-324-0405

Ocean Graphics
200A Springs Fireplace Road
631-329-1220
www.oceangraphicsigns.com

UPS Business Center
81 Newtown Lane
631-907-1100

Montauk

Montauk Printing & Graphics
771 Montauk Highway
631-668-3333

Southampton

Dunkerly's Office Products
137 Main Street
631-283-9080

East End Computers
50 Hill Street
631-725-4000
info@eastendcomputers.com

Hampton Copy
190 David Whites Lane
631-287-3135
www.hamptoncopy.com

Wainscott

Computer Professionals
41 Industrial Road
631-537-9888
www.cpeh.info

Water Mill

East End Blueprints & Reprographics
670 Montauk Hwy
631-726-2583
www.eeblue.com

PROPANE GAS

Bay Gas Co.
27 McGraw Street – Shirley
631-399-3620
www.baygasservice.com

Blue Light Energy
2823 Montauk Hwy - Bridgehamtpon
631-537-0668
www.hamptonspropane.com

East Hampton Fuel
14 Washington Ave
631-324-2420
www. hamptonshomeheatingoil.com

Johns Gas Service
PO Box 423 – Shelter Island
631-749-0195
www.johnsgas.com

Hampton Tank Gas Service
77 Maple Lane - Bridgehampton
631-537-0297

Piccozzi's Propane Service
177 N. Ferry Road – Shelter Island Heights
631-749-0045

Pulver Gas
2339 Montauk Hwy - Bridgehampton
631-537-0930

Schenck Fuels
62 Newtown Lane – East Hampton
631-324-0142
www.schenckfuels.com

Suburban Propane
233 Butter Lane – Bridgehampton
631-537-0930
www.suburbanpropane.com

W.C. Esp
2141 Main Street - Bridgehampton
631-537-0193
www.wcesp.com

REAL ESTATE OFFICES

Bespoke Realty
www.bespokerealestate.com
Water Mill
631-500-9030

Brown Harris Stevens
www.bhshamptons.com
-Bridgehampton
631-537-2727
-East Hampton
631-324-6400
-Sag Harbor
631-725-2250
-Southampton
631-287-4900

Compass
www.compass.com/hamptons
-Bridgehampton (Regional Office)
631-537-7700
-East Hampton
631-324-1700
-Southampton
631-259-9993
-Sag Harbor
631-725-2626
-Montauk
631-668-2000

Corcoran
www.corcoran.com/hamptons
-Amagansett
631-267-3900
-Bridgehampton
631-537-3900
-East Hampton
631-324-3900
-Montauk
631-668-3500
-Sag Harbor
631-725-1500
-Shelter Island
631-749-1600
-Southampton
631-283-7300

Douglas Elliman
www.elliman.com
-Bridgehampton
631-537-5900
-East Hampton
631-329-9400
-Montauk
631-668-6565
-Sag Harbor
631-725-0200
-Sagaponack
631-537-0600
-Southampton
631-283-4343

Saunders & Associates
www.hamptonsrealestate.com
-Bridgehampton
631-537-5454
-East Hampton
631-324-7575
-Southampton
631-238-5050

Sotheby's
www.sothebyshomes.com/hamptons
-Bridgehampton
631-537-6000
-East Hampton
631-324-6000
-Sag Harbor
631-725-6000
-Southampton
631-283-0600

Town & Country
www.townandcountryhamptons.com
-Bridgehampton
631-537-3200
-East Hampton
631-324-8080
-Southampton
631-283-5800
-Montauk
631-668-0500

SEAMSTRESS/TAILOR

Modas Eva
69 Newtown Lane – East Hampton
631-329-5916

Nancy's Tailoring
3334 Noyac Road – Sag Harbor
631-725-1517

North Main Street Cleaners
120 N. Main – East Hampton
631-324-1640

Stitch
22 Nugent Street – Southampton
631-377-3993

Tony's Tailoring & Tuxedo
133 Main Street – Southampton
631-283-287-6311

Southampton Village Dry Cleaners
56 Jagger Lane – Southampton
631-283-2299

Water Mill Village Cleaners
760 Montauk Highway – Water Mill
631-726-6400

TOWING SERVICE

Fireplace Auto Collision
195 Springs Fireplace Road – East Hampton
631-907-9839

Hampton Auto Collision
847 Springs Fireplace – East Hampton
631-324-6969

Robs Towing & Transport Road Recovery
East Hampton & Surrounding Area
631-680-3947

Southampton Collision
154 Mariner Drive – Southampton
631-283-1889

VAV Classics
21 Plant St – Southampton
631-283-9409

TRAVEL

AUTO RENTALS

Budget Car Rental
639 County Rd 39 – Southampton
631-283-3057

East Hampton Airport
200 Daniels Hole Road – East Hampton
631-537-4800

Enterprise Rent-A-Car
395 County Rd 39 – Southampton
631-283-0055

Hertz
59 Maple St – Southampton
631-283-1584

Hertz-Corrigans
1640 Montauk Highway – Bridgehampton
631-537-3843

BUS

The Hampton Jitney & Ambassador
631-283-4600
www.hamptonjitney.com
www.hamptonambassador.com

Hampton Luxury Liner
631-537-5800
www.hamptonluxuryliner.com

CAR SERVICE

East End Limousine
631-726-7400
www.eastendlimousine.com

East Wind Limo Service
631-902-9621
www.ewlimo.com

Hamptons Limousine Service
631-655-1756
www.hamptonslimousineservice.com

Southampton Limousine
631-297-0001
www.southamptonlimo.com

Sunny Limo & Car Service
631-281-8800
www.sunnylimos.com

Twin Forks Limousine
631-287-2112 – Southampton
631-907-0002 – East Hampton
www.info@twinforkslimousine.com

FERRY

Cross Sound Ferry
Orient Point, NY - New London, CT
631-323-2525
www.longislandferry.com

The Bridgeport & Port Jefferson Steamboat Company
Port Jefferson, NY - Bridgeport, CT
1-888-44FERRY
www.88844ferry.com

Viking Fleet
Montauk, NY - Block Island, RI
631-668-5700
www.vikingfleet.com

TAXI SERVICE

Amagansett

Amagansett Taxi
631-267-2006

Bridgehampton

Midway Limo & Taxi Service
631-537-1800

East Hampton

Alex Taxi
631-324-2100
Bills Taxi
631-907-8688
East End Taxi
631-324-8800 or 631-324-0077
East Hampton Best Taxi
631-668-8144
Super Taxi East Hampton
631-903-5246
Taxi One Hamptons
631-871-9906
Ted's Taxi East Hampton
631-324-2003
Tejedor Taxi
631-830-7012

Montauk

668 Montauk Taxi Service
631-668-1040
Lindy's Taxi
631-668-8888
Montauk's Best Taxi
631-668-8444

Montauk Taxi
631-668-2468
Pink Tuna Taxi
631-668-3838

Southampton

Hometown Taxi
631-283-5200
Southampton Taxi
631-889-3647
Zoom Taxi Southampton
631-287-0008

Sag Harbor

Sag Harbor Car Service
631-725-9000

TRAIN

Long Island Railroad (L.I.R.R.)
East Hampton Station
718-217-5477
www.mta.info/lirr

BEACHES & BAYS

EAST HAMPTON BEACHES

Beach Parking Permits are required at all Town and Village Beaches beginning May 26 thru Labor Day.

East Hampton Township runs from Wainscott to Montauk Point

**BEACHES OPEN FULL-TIME/7 DAYS A WEEK
STARTING JUNE 23 – LABOR DAY.**

Rules:
• No alcoholic beverages
• No fires and/or barbeques
• Parks and beaches close at 9:00 pm
• No glass containers allowed
• Dogs are allowed on beaches before 9:00 am and after 6:00 pm and must be on a leash

**Town of East Hampton Beach Parking Permits are not valid at East Hampton Village Beaches and Village permits are not valid at town beaches.

Some beaches sell daily parking spots — **noted below.**

VILLAGE OCEAN BEACHES

Village Parking permits available at East Hampton Village Hall -
86 Main Street – 631-324-4150

• Beach passes are free to village Residents
• Non-resident passes available for $400/vehicle - Limited supply available
•Village resident permit required May 15 - September 15
• Lifeguards on **3 village beaches** daily from 10:00 am- 5:00 pm

Egypt Beach – 55 Old Beach Lane

Georgica Beach – 219 Lily Pond Lane
Lifeguard, restrooms, showers

Main Beach – 101 Ocean Avenue
Lifeguard, restrooms, showers, concession stand, **daily permits sold $30/day on weekdays**

Two Mile Hollow Beach – 50 Two Mile Hollow Road
Lifeguard, quiet, **daily parking permits sold $30/day on weekdays**

Wiborg Beach – 74 Highway Behind the Pond

TOWN OCEAN BEACHES

Town Parking permits available at East Hampton Town Hall
159 Pantigo Rd - 631-324-2417

- Beach passes are free to Town Residents
- Non-resident passes available for $400/vehicle.
- Town permits for parking are required 24/7, 365 days per year
- Lifeguards on duty where noted from 10:00 am – 5:00 pm

Atlantic Avenue Beach – 4 Atlantic Avenue - Amagansett
Daily parking permits sold $25/day, restrooms, showers, concession stand, lifeguard, dogs allowed on the left side of the lifeguard station daily, surf chair-physically challenged

Ditch Plains Beach - 10 Deforest Road- Montauk
Lifeguard, rest rooms, showers, mobile concession stand, surf chair-physically challenged, surfers, fishing, hiking

Edison Beach – S. Edison Street - Montauk
Lifeguard, rest rooms, surf chair-physically challenged, no concession, no parking

Indian Wells Beach – Indian Wells Highway – Amagansett
Lifeguard, rest rooms, mobile concession stand, volleyball, surf-chair physically challenged

Navahoe Lane Beach – Navahoe Lane – Amagansett
No lifeguard, no concession, no restroom, limited parking

Town Line Road – 30 Town Line Road – Wainscott
No lifeguard, no concession, no restrooms, limited parking

EAST HAMPTON BAY BEACHES

Town Parking Permits required:

Barnes Hole Beach - Barnes Hole Road – Amagansett

Big Alberts Landing - Alberts Landing Road -Amagansett
Lifeguard, rest rooms, BBQ grills, picnic tables

East Lake Beach (Gin Beach) - East Lake Drive – Montauk Lifeguard, rest rooms, concession stands, surf chair-physically challenged

Fresh Pond Beach – Fresh Pond Road -Napeague Bay
Rest rooms, BBQ grills, picnic tables, tether ball, nature hiking trails, no lifeguard, no concession

Gerard Beach – Gerard Lane – Springs
Kayaking, Paddle boarding

Lazy Point Beach – 150 Lazy Point Road – Napeague Bay accessed through Napeague State Park
Paddle boarding, Kayak, boat launch

Louse Point – Louse Point Road – Springs
Paddle boarding, Kayak, boat launch, fishing

Maidstone Park Beach – Flaggy Hole Road - Springs
Lifeguard, rest rooms, picnic area, grills, playground, fishing off the jetty, hiking, beautiful sunsets

Mile Hill Beach – Mile Hill Road – East Hampton

Navy Beach – Navy Beach Road – Montauk

Old House Landing – Old House Landing Road – East Hampton
Quiet, good for kayak and paddle board launch

Sammy's Beach – Sammy's Beach Road – East Hampton
Limited parking, good hiking

West Lake Beach – West Lake Drive – Montauk
Restrooms, concession, launching ramp

SOUTHAMPTON BEACHES

Beach Parking Permits are required at all Town Beach Recreation Facilities beginning May 26 thru Labor Day. They can be purchased throughout the season at Parks & Recs.

Southampton Township runs from Remsenburg to Georgica Pond

BEACHES OPEN FULL-TIME/7 DAYS A WEEK STARTING JUNE 23 – LABOR DAY.

Rules:
• No alcoholic beverages
• No fires and/or barbeques – special permits are available at parks & recs and can be used after 6:00 pm
• Parks and beaches close at 9:00 pm
• No glass containers allowed
• Swimming in protected areas only
• Dogs are allowed on beaches before 9:00 am and after 6:00 pm and must be on a leash
• Lifeguards on duty 10:00 am – 5:00 pm

**Town of Southampton Beach Parking Permits are not valid at Southampton Village Beaches

Some beaches sell daily parking spots — **noted below.**

VILLAGE OCEAN BEACHES

Village Parking permits available at Village Hall –
23 Main Street, Southampton 631-283-0247
treasurer@southamptonvillage.org

• Beach passes are available for Village Residents or year round village renters free of charge
• Local Non-resident year round $225/vehicle
• Summer Visitors $350/vehicle

Coopers Beach – 268 Meadow Lane
Ocean beach, **daily parking permits sold $40/day,** rest rooms, showers, umbrella rentals, chair rentals, concession stand, voted most beautiful beach in the USA

Cryder Beach – 17 Cryder Lane
Ocean beach, quiet, no restrooms, no lifeguard

Dune Beach – 1992 Meadow Lane
Ocean beach, rest rooms, quiet

Fowler Beach – 1 Fowler Street
Ocean beach, no restrooms, no lifeguard

Gin Lane – Gin Lane -Parking in front of Southampton Bathing Corp
& St Andrews Dune Church
Ocean beach, no restrooms, no lifeguard

Halsey Neck Lane – Intersection of Halsey Neck Land & Gin Lane
Ocean Beach, no lifeguard, porta potties installed in the summer

Little Plains Beach – 258 Meadow Lane
Ocean beach, no lifeguard, porta potties installed in the summer

Old Town Beach – Intersection of Old Town Rd & Gin Lane
Ocean beach, no lifeguard, porta potties installed in the summer

Wyandanch – Intersection of Wyandanch Lane & Gin Lane
Ocean beach, no lifeguard, porta potties installed in the summer

TOWN OCEAN BEACHES

**Town Parking permits available at the Parks & Recreation
Office : 631-728-8585**
www.southamptontownny.gov

•Beach passes are available for town Residents or year round
   renters for $40/vehicle.
• Non-resident passes available for $375/vehicle.
• Full-season permits are required at all Town/Trustee access roads
from July 1 – Labor Day.

Flying Point Beach –1055 Flying Point Road - Water Mill Ocean
beach, life guard, rest rooms, showers, mobile concession stand,
surfers

Foster Memorial Long Beach –1000 Long Beach Road – Noyac –
Sag Harbor
Bay beach, lifeguard, rest rooms, **separate section on the left with
no parking permit required**

Mecox Beach – 535 Jobs Lane - Bridgehampton
Ocean beach, **daily parking permits sold $25/day,** lifeguard, restrooms, showers, snack bar, families

Sagg Main Beach – 315 Surfside Drive - Sagaponack
Ocean beach, **daily parking permits sold $25/day,** lifeguard, restrooms, showers, mobile concession stand, great spot for beach picnics and BBQ'S.

Scott Cameron Beach – 425 Dune Road - Bridgehampton
Ocean beach, lifeguard, showers, rest rooms, good body surfing

SAG HARBOR   BEACHES
Village Permit Required:

Village Municipal Building
55 Main Street ,Sag Harbor 631-725-0222

- Resident: FREE but a sticker is mandatory
- Non Resident: $100 per year for a sticker
- Daily Passes: $10 per car per day

Havens Beach – 1 Havens Lane
Bay beach, lifeguard, rest rooms, picnic tables, playground, dog park

No Permit Required:

Essex Street Beach – Essex Street - Montauk
Ocean beach, quite

Fowler Beach – Fowler Lane - Southampton
Ocean beach, little parking, quiet

Hither Hills State Park – Montauk
Ocean beach next to Hither Hills State Park camping grounds, reservations required for camping, parking available for a fee, good for families

Kirk Park Beach – Main Street - Montauk
Ocean beach, close to town, quiet, good for families, lifeguard, rest rooms, concessions

ENTERTAINMENT

MOVIE THEATRES

UA East Hampton 6
30 Main Street - East Hampton
631-324-0448

UA Southampton
43 Hill Street - Southampton
844-462-7342

UA Hampton Bays
119 W. Montauk Hwy - Hampton Bays
631-728-8676

THEATRE

Bay Street Theatre
Long Wharf - Sag Harbor
631-725-9500
www.baystreet.org

John Drew Theatre/Guild Hall
158 Main Street - East Hampton
631-324-4050
www.guildhall.org

Suffolk Theatre
118 E. Main Street – Riverhead
631-727-4343
www.suffolktheatre.com

Southampton Cultural Center
25 Pond Lane – Southampton
631-287-4377
www.scc-arts.org

Westhampton Beach Performing Arts Center
76 Main Street - Westhampton
631-288-1500
www.whbpac.org

LIVE MUSIC & CLUBS
Amagansett

The Stephen Talkhouse
161 Main Street
631-267-3117
www.stephentalkhouse.com

East Hampton

Miss Chloe
44 Three Mile Harbor Road
631-324-3332

Montauk

Memory Motel
692 Main Street
631-668-2702

Navy Beach
16 Navy Road
631-668-6868
www.navybeach.com/restaurant

Rushmeyers
161 Second House Road
www.ruschmeyersmtk.com

Saltbox
99 Carl Fisher Plaza
631-238-5727
www.montauksaltbox.com

Shagwong Tavern
774 Montauk Highway
631-668-3050
Tuesday & Thurday: DJ
Friday & Saturday: Live Music
www.shagwongtavern.com

Surf Lodge
183 Edgemere Street
631-238-5216
www.surflodgemontauk.com

The Sloppy Tuna
148 South Emerson Avenue
631-647-8000
www.thesloppytuna.com

Sagaponack

Townline BBQ
3393 Townline road
631-537-2271
www.townlinebbq.com

Wolffer Estate (on Fridays)
139 Sagg Road
631-537-5107
www.wolffer.com

Sag Harbor

Bay Burger (Jazz Jam on Thursdays)
1742 Bridge-Sag Turnpike
631-899-3915
www.bayburger.com

Barons Cove
31 West Water Street
844-227-6672
www.baronscove.com

Lulu's
126 Main Street
631-725-0900
Thursdays: 6:00-9:00 p.m.
www.lulusagharobor.com

M.J. Dowlings
3360 Noyac Road
631-725-4444
Open Mic : 8:00 – 11 p.m. Wednesdays
Karaoke: 10:00 – 1:00 a.m. Fridays
www.mjdowlings.com

Southampton

A.M. Southampton
125 Tuckahoe Lane
516-492-0346
www.Amsouthampton.com

Coast Grill
1109 Noyac Road
631-283-2277
Fridays: 8:00 p.m.
www.thecoastgrillrestaurant.com

North Sea Tavern
1271 North Sea Road
631-353-3322
www.northseatavern.com

Union Cantina
40 Bowden Square
631-377-3500
www.unioncantina.net

75 Main
75 Main Street
631-283-7575
www.75main.com

FARM STANDS & FARMER'S MARKETS

Amagansett

Amber Waves Farm
375 Main St

Balsam Farms
284 Town Ln

Vicki's Veggies
597 Montauk Hwy

Bridgehampton

Babinski/Comfort Farm Stand
791 Lumber Lane
June - October 10:00 a.m. – 8:00 p.m.

Fairview Farm
69 Horsemill Lane
May – October 10:00 a.m. – 6:00 p.m.

Hayground School Farmers Market
151 Mitchells Ln
Fridays 3PM -6:30PM

Mecox Bay Dairy
855 Mecox Rd

Open Minded Organics
720 Butter Ln

East Hampton

Bhumi Farm
139 Pantigo Rd

37

Dayton Farms at Hardscrabble
Rt 114 & Stephen Hands Path
July - October

East Hampton Farmer's Market - Nick & Toni's parking
136 N. Main St
Fridays 9AM – 1PM

EECO Farm Stand
55 Long Lane

Iacono Farm
92 Long Lane

Pantigo Farm Co
390 Pantigo Rd

Round Swamp Farm
184 Three Mile Harbor Rd

Spring Close Farm Stand & Nursery
92 Spring Close Highway

Springs Farmer's Market - Ashawagh Hall
780 Springs Fireplace Rd
Saturdays 9AM-1PM

Montauk

Montauk Farmer's Market – Village Green
5 Greenfield Drive
Thursdays 9AM – 2PM

Sagaponack

Pike Farms
82 Sagg Main St
June – October 9:00 a.m. – 6:00 p.m.

Sag Harbor

Sag Harbor Farmer's Market
Bay St & Burke St
Saturday 9AM – 1PM

Serene Green
3980 Noyac Road

Shelter Island

Havens' Farmer's Market
16 S. Ferry Rd
Saturday 9AM – 12:30PM

The Shelter Island Farm Stand / Sep's Farm
87 N. Ferry Road
June – Labor Day Weekend

Southampton

Hanks Farmstand
324 County Rd 39
U Pick strawberries – June ; raspberries & blueberries Jul/August

North Sea Farms
1060 Noyac Rd

Southampton Farmer's Market
25 Jobs Lane
Sundays 9AM-2PM

Wainscott

Lisa & Bill's Fresh Vegetables (Babinski Farm)
Main Street & Beach Lane

Water Mill

Babinski's Farm Stand
160 Newlight Ln, Water Mill

Country Garden Farm Stand
35 Millstone Rd, Water Mill

Fairview Farm at Mecox
69 Horsemill Lane

Green Thump Organic Farm
829 Montauk Hwy

Halsey Farmstand & Nursery
513 Deerfield Road

The Milk Pail
1346 Montauk Hwy
Open Year Round – every day EXCEPT Tuesday

FITNESS

KICK BOXING

Mark Tuthill's Martial Arts Center
37 Three Mile Harbor Rd – East Hampton
www.marktuthill.com

PILATES
Amagansett

Peerless Pilates
532 Montauk Hwy
516-455-2347

Bridgehampton

Bridgehampton Pilates
2273 Montauk Hwy
631-537-5144
www.bridgehamptonpilates.net

East Hampton

The Body Shop
26 Newtown Lane
631-324-6440
www.thebodyshopeasthampton.com

Bradford Method
58 Gingerbread Ln
631-213-9413
www.bradfordmethod.com

Elements Fitness
68 Newtown Lane, #6
631-604-5445
www.elementsfitnessstudio.com

Erika Bloom Pilates
66 Newtown Lane, #7
631-288-3410
www.erikabloompilates.com

Pilates By Hamptons Gym
1 Railroad Avenue
631-324-5653

Silich Core + Strength
79 Newtown Lane
631-767-2709
www.silichcore.com

SLT East Hampton
460 Pantigo Rd, Unit 1
212-355-1737
www.sltnyc.com/#home

Well Within
135 Springs Fireplace Rd
www.wellwithinstudio.com

Montauk

New York Pilates
649 Montauk Hwy
www.newyorkpilates.com

Sag Harbor

In Balance Pilates Studio
34 W. Water St.
631-725-8282
www.inbalancestudio.com

Norma Jean Pilates
52 Main St
631-235-0303
www.normajeanpilates.com

The Pilates Method
74 Main Street
631-725-7995

Pilates of Sag Harbor
74 Main St
631-725-7995
www.PilatesOfSagHarbor.com

Uptown Pilates
23 Bridge Street
631-725-5994
www.uptownpilates.com/home-2/sag-harbor

Shelter Island

Shelter Island Pilates
8 Grand Ave
631-749-5042
www.shelterislandpilates.com

Wainscott

Le Petit Studio
354 Montauk Hwy, Lift Hampton - Wainscott
631-610-1524
www.lepetitstudionyc.com

Water Mill

Water Mill Pilates
58 Deerfield Rd - Water Mill
631-835-2281
www.watermillpilates.net

SPINNING
Amagansett

B East
199 Main Street
631-267-0900
www.eastfit.com

43

Bridgehampton

SoulCycle
264 Butter Lane
631-537-3630
www.soul-cycle.com

East Hampton

Flywheel
65 Montauk Highway Suite C
631-329-8622

SoulCycle
68 Newtown Lane
631-324-6600
www.soul-cycle.com

Montauk

SoulCycle
15 S. Edgemere St.
www.soulcycyle.com

Swerve @ the Surf Club
20 Surfside Ave
www.swervefitness.com

Sag Harbor

Flywheel
1 Bay Street - Sag Harbor
631-899-4256
www.new-york.flywheelsports.com

Water Mill

SoulCycle
760 Montauk Hwy
631-324-6610
www.soul-cycle.com

STUDIOS & GYMS
Amagansett

Barry's Bootcamp
199 Main Street
631-267-3015

Body Tech
249 Main Street
631-267-8222
www.bodytechclub.com

Bridgehampton

Exhale Core Fusion
2415 Main St
www.exhalespa.com

Physique 57
264 Butter Ln
www.physique57.com

Gotham Gym
2405 Montauk Hwy
www.gothamgymnyc.com

East Hampton

AKT in Motion
3 Railroad Ave
www.aktinmotion.com

E.H. Gym
2 Fithian Lane
631-324-4499
www.hamptonsgymcorp.com

Jamie Lerner Fitness & Dance
26 Newtown Lane
631-604-1462
www.jamielerner.com

MuvStrong
289 Springs Fireplace Road
631-527-5755
www.muvstrong.com

Truth Training
5 Railroad Ave
www.truthtraining.com

YMCA
2 Gingerbread Lane
631-329-6884
www.ymcali.org/East-Hampton

Montauk

Bari Studio
183 Edgemere Street
www.thebaristudio.com

Gurneys
290 Old Montauk Hwy
631-668-2345
www.gurneysinn.com/sea-water-spa

Sag Harbor

Punch Fitness
89 Clay Pit Rd
www.punchfitnesscenter.com

Sag Harbor Gym
1 Bay Street
631-725-0707
www.hamptonsgymcorp.com

Southampton

Barry's Bootcamp
10 Montauk Hwy
631-353-3833
www.barrysbootcamp.com

Brownings Fitness
60 Windmill Lane
315-955-6989
www.browningsfitness.com

CrossFit Hamptons
375 County Road 39
631-276-5820
www.cfhamptons.com

East End Row
33 Hill St
wwweastendrow.com

Omni Health & Racquet Club
395 Country Road
631-283-4770
www.hamptons

Pure Barre
5 Windmill Ln
www.purebarre.com

SLT
16 Hill St
www.slnyc.com

Wainscott

Barry's Bootcamp
352 Montauk Hwy
631-537-2668
www.barrysbootcamp.com

Lift Hampton
354 Montauk Hwy
631-604-2558
*by appointment only

Water Mill

Tracy Anderson
903 Montauk Hwy
www.tracyanderson.com

YOGA
Amagansett

Mandala Yoga
249 Main Street
631-267-6144
www.mandalayoga.com

Bridgehampton

Hamptons Hot Yoga
2415 Montauk Hwy
631-537-9642
www.hamptonshotyoga.com

One Ocean Yoga
1927 Scuttle Hole Rd
www.onceoceanyoga.com

East Hampton

JB Yoga & KamaDeva Yoga
15 Lumber Ln, 2nd Floor
www.kamadevayoga.com

Montauk

BYoga
83 South Elwood Ave
www.byogahive.com

Yoga Lila
12 South Edna Ave
www.yogalilamontuak.com

Sag Harbor

Yoga Shanti
32 Bridge Street
631-725-6424
www.yogashanti.com

Shelter Island

Shelter Island Yoga & Fitness
13 Winthrop Rd
631-749-0160
www.shelterislandyog.org

HOUSE CALLS

Claudia Matles
Yoga, Pilates, Nutrition
Private and Group sessions
631-721-7515
www.claudiamatles.com

FOOD & PARTY STUFF

BAGLES

Bagel Buoy
3 Bay Street – Sag Harbor
631-725-7690

Bagel Palace
40 Montauk Highway – Southampton
631-723-1086

Goldberg's Famous Bagels
2123 Montauk Highway – Bridgehampton
631-296-8110
100 Pantigo Place – East Hampton
631-329-8300
28 S. Etna Ave – Montauk
631-238-5976
2101 Montauk Highway – Napeague
631-267-5552
801 County Road 39 – Southampton
631-204-1046
358 Montauk Highway – Wainscott
631-537-5553

Hampton Bagels
74 N. Main Street – East Hampton
631-324-5411

BAKERIES

Blue Duck Bakery & Cafe
30 Hampton Road – Southampton
631-204-1701

Breadzilla
84 Wainscott NW Road – Wainscott
631-537-0955

Carissa's Breads
68 Newtown Lane – East Hampton
631-329-3993

Kyle's
27 N. Ferry Road – Shelter Island
631-749-0579

Left Hand Coffee & Bakery
57 Flamingo Avenue – Montauk
631-238-5434

Levain Bakery
354 Montauk Highway – Wainscott
631-537-8570

Marie Eiffel
184 N. Ferry Road – Shelter Island
631-749-0003

Montauk Bake Shoppe
29 Carl Fisher Plaza – Montauk
631-668-2439

Pierre's Patisserie
2468 Main Street – Bridgehampton
631-537-5110

Sag Harbor Baking Company
51 Division Street – Sag Harbor
631-899-4900

Sant Ambroeus
30 Main Street – Southampton
631-283-1233

Tate's Bake Shop
43 N. Sea Road – Southampton
631-283-9830

Ye Olde Bake Shoppe
17 Windmill Lane – Southampton
631-283-6553

BUTCHERS

Catena's Market
143 Main Street – Southampton
631-283-3456

Citarella
2209 Montauk Highway – **Bridgehampton**
2 Pantigo Road – **East Hampton**
20 Hampton Road – **Southampton**
631-283-6600

Cromer's Country Market
3500 Noyac Road – Sag Harbor
631-725-9004

Dean's Country Market
214 Mill Road – Westhampton
631-288-5532

Hampton Marketplace
36 Race Lane – East Hampton
631-329-7000

Justin's Chop Shop
214 Mill Road – Westhampton
631-288-5532

Peconic Prime Meats
235 North Sea Road – Southampton
631-488-4697

Schiavoni's Market
48 Main Street – Sag Harbor
631-725-0366

Scotto's Italian Pork Store
25 West Montauk Highway – Hampton Bays
631-728-5677

Villa Italian Specialties
7 Railroad Ave – East Hampton
631-324-5110

Village Prime Meat Shop
495 Montauk Highway – East Quogue
631-653-8071

CHEESE SHOPS

Breadzilla
84 Wainscott NW Road – Wainscott
631-537-0955

Cavaniola's Gourmet Cheese Shop
89B Division Street -Sag Harbor
631-725-0095
AND:
8 Amagansett Square - Amagansett
631-267-5608
www.cavaniolas.com

The Village Gourmet Cheese Shoppe
11 Main Street – Southampton
631-283-7951
www.villagecheeseshoppe.com

CLAMBAKES

Amagansett Seafood Store
501 Montauk Highway – Amagansett
631-267-6015

Bobs Fish Market
87 North Ferry Rd - Shelter Island
631-749-0830
www.fritosandfoiegras.com

Citarella
2 Pantigo Road - East Hampton
2209 Montauk Hwy – Bridgehampton
20 Hampton Road – Southampton
631-283-6600
www.citarella.com

Clam Man Seafood Market
235A N. Sea Road - Southampton
631-283-3354

Claws on Wheels
17 Race Lane - East Hampton
631-324-9224
www.edibleeastend.com

East End Clambakes
590 North Hwy - Southampton
631-726-5360
www.eastendclambakes.com

Hampton Clam Bake
39 Gann Road - East Hampton
631-324-8620
www.hamptonclambake.com

The Seafood Shop
356 Montauk Highway – Wainscott
631-537-0633
www.theseafoodshop.com

Stuart's Seafood Market
41 Oak Lane – Amagansett
631-267-6700
www.stuartsseafood.com

COUNTRY MARKETS & DELI'S

Amagansett

Amber Waves Farm Market
375 Montauk Highway

Brent's General Store
8 Montauk Highway
631-267-3113

Bridgehampton

Bridgehampton Town Deli
2450 Main Street
631-537-3011

Mickey B's Deli
173 Bridgehampton-Sag Harbor Turnpike
631-537-1114

Round Swamp Farm
97 School Street
631-324-4428

East Hampton

Barnes Country Store
716 Springs Fireplace Road
631-324-4790

Bucket's Deli
107 Newtown Lane
631-324-0747

Damark's Deli & Market
331 Three Mile Harbor Road
631-324-0691

Hampton Market Place
36 Race Lane
631-329-7000

Maidstone Market & Deli
514 Three Mile Harbor Road
631-329-2830

Old Stone Market
472 Old Stone Highway
631-267-6244

One Stop Market
293 Springs Fireplace Road
631-324-6055

Red Horse Market
74 Montauk Highway
631-324-9500

Round Swamp Farm
184 Three Mile Harbor Road
631-324-4438

Springs General Store
29 Old Stone Highway
631-329-5065

Villa Italian Specialties
7 Railroad Avenue
631-324-5110

Montauk

Embassy Market
S Embassy & Euclid Street
631-668-2323

Four Oaks Gourmet Deli
57 Flamingo Avenue
631-668-2534

Four Oaks Montauk Market
805 Montauk Highway
631-668-1689

Gaviola's Montauk Market
West Lake Drive & Wells Avenue
631-668-1031

Gin Beach Market
541 East Lake Drive
631-668-3088

Herbs Market
778 Montauk Highway
631-668-2335

Ricks Food Service
231 Essex Street
631-668-4619

The Market
463 W. Lake Drive
631-238-5433

Sagaponack

Loave & Fishes
50 Sagg Main Street
631-537-0555

Pierre's Market
542 Sagg Main Street
631-297-8400

Sag Harbor

Cove Deli
283 Main Street
631-725-0216

Cromer's Country Market
3500 Noyac Road
631-725-9004

Espresso da asporto
2 Main Street
631-725-5668

Harbor Market & Kitchen
184 Division Street
631-725-4433

Jimmy Jims Deli
3348 Noyac Road
631-725-1930

Provisions
7 Main Street
631-725-3636

Shelter Island

Fedi's Deli
43 State Road
631-749-1177

Marie Eiffel Market
184 N. Ferry Road
631-749-0003

Southampton

Catena's Market
143 Main Street
631-283-3456

Country Deli
926 Noyac Road
631-283-4900

Dejesus Deli Grocery
376 County Road 39
631-488-4100

Fresco Pizza Deli
623 Hampton Road
631-259-2987

North Sea General Store
1360 North Sea Road
631-283-1826

Sean's Place
54 Hampton Road
631-283-6266

Schmidt Brothers Produce
120 North Sea Road
631-283-5777

South Fork Deli
863 County Road 39
631-283-3130

Ted's East End Market
264 Hampton Road
631-283-0929

Water Mill

The Deli at Water Mill
670 Montauk Highway
631-726-3354

FISH MARKETS
Amagansett

Amagansett Seafood Shop
501 Montauk Highway
631-267-6015

Multi Aquaculture Systems
429 Cranberry Hole Road
631-267-3341

Stuarts Seafood
41 Oak Lane
631-267-6700

Bridgehampton

Round Swamp Farm
97 School Street
631-324-4428

Citarella
2209 Montauk Hwy
631-283-6600
www.citarella.com

East Hampton

Citarella
2 Pantigo Road
631-283-6600
www.citarella.com

Claws on Wheels
17 Race Lane
631-324-5090

Dreeson's Catering
15 Lumber Lane
631-324-0465

Fish 27 Seafood Market
299 Pantigo Road
631-324-1100

Montauk

Dureya's Lobster Deck
65 Tuthill Road
631-668-2410

Gossman's Fish Market
484 West Lake Drive
631-668-5645

St. Peter's Catch
58 S. Erie Ave
631-668-7100

Sagaponack

Loaves & Fishes
50 Sagg Main Street
631-537-0555

Shelter Island

Bob's Fish Market
87 N. Ferry Road
631-749-0830

Fish Hawk Seafood
3 North Ferry Road
631-749-5777

Southampton

Catena's Food Market
143 Main Street
631-283-3456

Citarella
20 Hampton Road
631-283-6600
www.citarella.com

Clamman Seafood Market
235A North Sea Road
631-283-6669

Cor-J Seafood
36 Lighthouse Road
631-728-5186

Schmidt's
1282 North Sea Road
631-283-1212

Tully's Seafood Market
78 Foster Avenue
631-728-9043

Wainscott

The Seafood Shop
356 Montauk Highway
631-537-0633

GROCERY STORES

Amagansett

Amagansett IGA
511 Montauk Highway
631-267-3556

Bridgehampton

Citarella
2209 Montauk Highway
631-283-6600

King Kullen
2044 Montauk Highway – Bridgehampton Commons
631-537-2681

East Hampton

Citarella
2 Pantigo Road
631-324-6600

East Hampton IGA
92 N. Main Street
631-324-0529

Stop & Stop
67 Newtown Lane
631-324-6215

Montauk

IGA
654 Montauk Highway
631-668-4929

Montauk Market
805 Montauk Highway
631-668-2071

Sag Harbor

Provisions
7 Main Street
631-725-3636

Schiavonis
48 Main Street
631-725-0366

Shelter Island

Shelter Island IGA
75 N. Ferry Road
631-740-0382

Southampton

Citarell
20 Hampton Road
631-283-6600

Stop & Shop
167 Main Street
631-283-0045

Waldbaums
23 Jagger Lane
631-283-0045

WINE, LIQUOR & BEVERAGE STORES

Amagansett

Amagansett Wine & Spirits
203 Main Street
631-267-3939

Atlantic Wine & Spirits
517 Montauk Highway
631-267-6330

Bridgehampton

DePetris Liquor Store
2489 Main Street
631-537-0287

McNamara Liquor
2102 Montauk Highway – Bridgehampton Commons
631-537-1230

East Hampton

Domain Franey Wines & Spirits
459 Pantigo Road
631-324-0906

East Hampton Wine & Spirits
293 Springs Fireplace Road
631-324-5757

Park Place Wines and Liquors
84 Park Place
631-324-2622

Race Lane Liquors
21 Race Lane
631-324-4595

Sam's Beverage Place
29 Race Lane
631-324-7267

Springs Wines & Liquors
839 Springs Fireplace Road
631-324-0322

Wines by Morrell
74 Montauk Highway
631-324-1230

Montauk

Finest Kind Wines & Liquors
552 W. Lake Drive
631-668-9463

Montauk Beer & Soda
43 S. Elmwood Ave
631-880-4503

Montauk Liquors & Wines
29 Carl Fisher Plaza
631-668-5454

Whites Liquor Store
711 Montauk Highway
631-668-2426

Sag Harbor

Cavaniola's Cellar
89A Division Street
631-725-2930

Long Wharf Wines & Spirits
12 Bay Street
631-725-2400

Noyac Liquors
3354 Noyac Road
631-725-0330

Sag Harbor Liquor
52 Main Street
631-725-0054

Sag Harbor Beverage
89 Division Street
631-725-7308

Water Street Wines & Spirits
2224 Long Island Ave
631-725-9178

Shelter Island

Dandy Liquors
43 N. Ferry Road
631-749-3302

Shelter Island Wines & Spirits
179 N. Ferry Road
631-749-0305

Southampton

Bottle Hampton
850 County Road 39
631-353-3315

Herbert & Rist
63 Jobs Lane
631-283-2030

Lamplighter Wines & Liquor
28 Jagger Lane
631-283-0158

North Sea Liquor
1272 N. Sea Road
631-283-5855

Peconic Beverage
79 County Road 39
631-283-0602

Zabi's Wines & Spirits
74 County Road 39
631-287-7171

Wainscott

Wainscott Main Wine & Spirits
354 Montauk Highway
631-537-2800

Water Mill

Southampton Wines at Water Mill
760 Montauk Highway
631-726-2712

PARTY RENTALS

ABC Party & Tent Rentals
631-256-5263

Bar Boy Products East
218 W. Montauk Highway – Hampton Bays
631-728-7100

Bermuda Party Rentals
5 Osborne Lane – East Hampton
631-324-7767

Party Rental Ltd.
50 Station Road -Water Mill
Unit #2
201-727-4706

Southampton Party Rentals
631-807-7627

The Party Shoppe
82 Park Place – East Hampton
631-324-9547

GALLERIES

Amagansett

Ille Arts
171 Main Street
631-905-9894
www.illearts.com

Neoteric Fine Art
68A Schellinger Road
631-838-7518
www.neotericfineart.com

Bridgehampton

Chase Edwards Fine Art
2462 Main Street
631-604-2204
www.chaseedwardsgallery.com

Elaine Benson Gallery
376 Bridgehampton-Sag Harbor Turnpike
Childrens Museum of the East End
631-537-8250
www.elainebensongallery.com

Julian Beck Fine Paintings
2454 Montauk Hwy
631-613-6200
www.julianbeck.com

Kathryn Market Fine Arts
2418 Montauk Hwy
631-613-6386
www.marketfinearts.com

Lucille Khornak Gallery
2400 Montauk Hwy
631-631-6000
www.lucillekhornak.com

Mark Borghi Fine Art
2426 Main Street
631-537-7245
www.borghi.org

RJD Gallery
2385 Main Street
631-725-1161
www.rjdgallery.com

The White Room Gallery
2415 Main Street
631-237-1481
www.thewhiteroom.gallery

East Hampton

Birnamwood Galleries
48 Park Place
631-324-6010
www.birnamwoodart.com

Casterline-Goodman Gallery
46 Newtown Lane
631-527-5525
www.Casterlinegoodman.com

Drawing Room
66 Newtown Lane
631-324-5016
www.drawingroomsgallery.com

Eric Firestone Gallery
4 Newtown Lane
631-604-2386
www.ericfirestonegallery.com

FolioEast
55 Main Street
917-592-8033
www.folioeast.com

Gallery Valentine
66 Newtown Lane
631-329-3100
www.galleryvalentine.com

Giraffics Gallery
79A Newtown Lane
631-329-0803
www.girafficsgallery.com

Halsey McKay Gallery
79 Newtown Lane
631-604-5770
www.halseymckay.com

Janet Lehr Fine Arts
68 Park Place
631-324-3303
www.janetlehrinc.com

Roman Fine Art
66 Park Place
917-797-8931
www.romanfineart.com

Wallace Gallery
37 Main Street
631-329-4516
Montauk

Montauk Artists Association
97 Edgemere Street
631-668-0897
www.montaukartistsassociation.org

Outeast Gallery and Goods
65 Tuthill Road
631-668-2376

Sag Harbor

Christy's Art Center
3 Madison Street
631-509-1379

Grenning Gallery
17 Washington Street
631-725-8469
www.grenninggallery.com

Monika Olko Galllery
95 Main Street
631-899-4740
www.monikaolkogallery.com

Romany Kramoris Gallery
41 Main Street
631-725-2499
www.kramorisgallery.com

Sara Nightingale Gallery
26 Main Street
631-793-2256
www.saranightingale.com

Tulla Booth Gallery
66 Main Street
631-725-3100
www.tullaboothgallery.com

Shelter Island

Boltax Gallery
21 N. Ferry Road
631-749-4062

Handwerklab Art Gallery
36 North Ferry Road
631-294-2765
www.handwerklab.com

Southampton

Arthur T. Kalaher Fine Art Gallery
28 Jobs Lane
631-283
Arthurkalaher@gmail.com

The Artists Study
25 Hampton Road
631-446-4404

Jeff Lincoln Art & Design
200 North Sea Road
631-353-3445
www.collectiveartdesign.com

Mark Humphrey Gallery
10 Jagger Lane
631-283-3113
www.markhumphreygallery.com

Raison Gallery
848 North Sea Road
631-276-6872
www.raisongallery.com

Stellar Union
25 N. Sea Road
631-204-0315
www.stellarunion.com

Todd Merrill Studio
11 South Main Street
631-259-3601
www.toddmerrillstudio.com

Tripoli Gallery
30A Jobs Lane
631-377-3715
www.tripoligallery.com

Water Mill

Celadon Gallery
41 Old Mill Road
631-726-2547
www.hamptonsclayart.org

Sara Nightingale Gallery
688 Montauk Highway
631-726-0076
www.saranightingale.com

HAIR & NAILS

HAIR SALONS

Amagansett

Salon & Day Spa @Amagansett Square
6 Amagansett Square
631-267-6677
www.amagansettsalonandspa.com

Water's Edge Salon
66542 Main Street
631-267-7766

Bridgehampton

Blow Hamptons
2422 Main Street
www.blowhampton.com

Fay Teller Salon
19 Corwith Ave
631-537-3393

Vincent Da Silva at Gil Ferrer Salon
2044 Montauk Hwy
631-537-5805
www.vincentferrersalon.com

East Hampton

Blow Hamptons
59 The Circle
631-324-8888
www.blowhampton.com

Special Effects
1 Osborne Lane
631-324-5996

Warren Tricomi Salon
64 Park Place
212-262-8899
www.warrentricomi.com

Montauk

Endz Salon
28 S. Edison St
631-668-5880
www.endzsalonmontauk.com

Pamela's New Beginning Salon
86 S. Euclid Ave
631-238-5525
www.montaukhairsalons.com

Gurney's Hairspace Salon
290 Old Montauk Hwy
631-668-2345
www.gurneysmontauk.com

Sag Harbor

Fingers Fine Haircutting
78 Main Street
631-725-1212
www.fingersfinehaircutting.com

Rave Hair Salon
3327 Noyac Rd
631-725-0948
www.ravehairsalon.com

Salon Xavier
1A Bay Street
631-725-6400
www.salonxavier.com

Scarlett Rose AVEDA Salon
80 Division Street
631-899-4949
www.scarlettrosesalon.com

Sean Edison Salon
34 W. Water Street
631-725-7326
www.seanedisonsalon.com

Shelter Island

Anna's Salon
69 N. Midway Rd
631-749-4293

Bonheur Supreme Spa
35 Shore Rd
440-253-9766
www.bonheursupremespa.com

Southampton

27 Hampton Salon
27 Hampton Rd
631-377-3107
www.27hamptonsalon.com

A.F.K Salon
20 Main Street
631-259-2444

Erin Downey Salon & Dry Studio
36 Hampton Rd
631-283-0644
www.erindowneysalons.com

Kevin Maple Salon
46 Jobs Lane
631-283-8230
www.thekevinmaplesalon.com

Revolve Hair
34 Hill Street
631-377-3555
www.revolvehair.com

NAIL SALONS

Amagansett

The Salon at Amagansett Square
6 Amagansett Square
631-267-6677
www.amagansettsalonandspa.com

Hampton Nails
195 Main Street
631-604-1885

Water's Edge Salon
538 Montauk Hwy
631-267-7766

Bridgehampton

Angel Tips Nail Spa
2102 Montauk Hwy
631-537-0100
www.angeltips.com

Fay Teller Salon
19 Corwith Ave
631-537-3393

East Hampton

Elegant Touch
1 Railroad Avenue
631-604-5444

Fresh Coat
8 Main Street
631-527-5766
info@freshcoatnails.com

Spa 27
65 Montauk Hwy
631-329-7868

Special Effects
1 Osborne Lane
631-324-5996
www.specialeffectsunisex.com

T-Nail
78 N. Main Street
631-324-2952

Warren Tricomi Salon
64 Park Place
212-262-8899
www.warrentricomi.com

Sag Harbor

D Nails Salon & Spa
2 Bay Street
631-725-8381

Salon Xavier
1A Bay Street
631-725-6400
www.salonxavier.com

Scarlett Rose AVEDA Salon of the Hamptons
80A Division Street
631-899-4949
www.scarlettrosesalon.com

Shelter Island

Bonheur Supreme Spa
35 Shore Rd
440-253-9766
www.bonheursupremespa.com

Southampton

Hampton Perfect Nail Salon
36 Hampton Rd
631-283-3877

Marcella Nails
10 Oak St
631-204-5200
www.marcellanails.com

Oceana Nail & Spa
9 Hill St
631-353-3669

Pure Nail & Spa
22 Jagger Lane
631-287-7200
www.purenailspany.com

Wainscott

Sweet Nails Salon
354 Montauk Hwy
631-537-9535

Water Mill

Serenity Nails
670 Montauk Hwy
631-726-4696

HOLISTIC HEALTH & DAY SPAS

ACUPUNCTURE

Dr. Eduardo Aversano
10 Main Street – **East Hampton**
631-804-7551
www.eduardoaversano.com

Bridgehampton Acupuncture
2230 Scuttlehole Road – **Sag Harbor**
631-537-8163
www.bridgehamptonacupuncture.com

Cirrone Wellness
50 Station Road, Bld. 7 – **Water Mill**
631-283-1300
www.drjanetcirrone.com

East End Acupuncture
43 Pantigo Road – **East Hampton**
631-329-5292
www.eastendacupuncture.com

Menard Acupuncture
39 Division Street – **Sag Harbor**
631-899-4112
www.menardacupuncutre.com

SGF Acupuncture
532 Montauk Highway – **Amagansett**
631-267-9500
www.SGFacupunture.com

DAY SPAS

Amagansett

The Salon at Amagansett Square
6 Amagansett Square
631-267-6677
www.amagansettsalonandspa.com

Bridgehampton

Blue Ocean Spa
2102 Montauk Hwy #112
631-537-0000
www.blueoceanspa.com

Exhale New York
2415 Main Street
212-561-6400
www.exhalespa.com

Palm Beach Cryo
42 Snake Hollow Road
631-296-8383
www.palmbeachcryotherapy.com

East Hampton

A.Studio Day Spa
10 Main St
631-324-6996
www.astudiodayspa.com

Baker House
181 Main St
631-324-4081
www.bakerhouse1650.com

J & G Wellness Enjoy Spa
61 The Circle
631-527-5257

Little Bird Spa
26 Park Pl
631-765-7742
www.littlebirdspa.com/easthampton

Naturopathica
74 Montauk Hwy
631-329-8792
www.naturopathica.com

Refresh Body (House Calls Only)
15 Wagon Lane
212-242-4379
www.refreshbody.com

Reverie Spa (House Calls Only)
84A Park Pl
631-324-4401
www.reveriespanyc.com

Salon Bar
66 Newtown Ln
631-604-5500
www.salonbar.com

Shape House
66 Newtown Lane
855-567-2346
www.theshapehouse.com

Spa 27
65 Montauk Hwy
631-329-7868
www.spa27.net

Montauk

Gurney's Seawater Spa
290 Old Montauk Hwy
631-668-2345
www.gurneysmontauk.com

Sag Harbor

Happy Feet
2 Division Street
631-808-3009
Salon Xavier
1 Bay Street
631-725-6400
www.salonxavier.com

Scarlett Rose/ Aveda
80 Division Street
631-899-4949
www.scarlettrosesalon.com

Southampton

Flying Point Spa
613 Route 27A
631-726-0650
www.flying-point-spa.buisness.site

Geomare Wellness Center & Spa
80 White Street
631-287-9352
www.geomarewellnesscenter.com

John Dillion Salon & Day Spa
16 Hill Street # 5
631-283-8383
www.johndillionsalonsh.com

Little Bird Spa
16 Hill Street #3
631-287-1118
www.littlebirdspa.com

Wainscott

La Don Spa
382 Montauk Hwy
631-604-6501
www.la-don.com

MEDITATION & HEALING CENTERS

Bridgehampton

Tapovana Ashtango
977 Bridgehampton Turnpike
631-678-3905
www.tapovana.com

East Hampton

Holistic Life Works
21 Cosdrew Lane
917-701-1105
www.holisticlifeworks.com

Well Within (House Calls Only)
135 Springs Fireplace Road
631-872-2133
www.wellwithinhamptons.com

Southampton

Joshua's Place
30 Sanford Place
631-287-2999
www.joshuasplace.org

Water Mill

Aegle Healing Center
50 Station Road, Bld 3 Unit 1
631-500-9021
www.aeglehealingcenter.com

Kadampa Meditation Center
720C Montauk Highway
631-728-5700
www.hamptonsmeditation.com

REIKI

The Healing Spring (House Calls Only)
Massage, Reflexology, Reiki
347-797-7755
www.thehealingspring.com

Inner Healing Arts
18 Seaside Ave – **Hampton Bays**
516-532-7633
www.innerhealingarts.com

Lauralee Kelly (House Calls Only)
646-823-4119
www.lauraleekelly.com

ALTERNATIVE HEALING METHODS

Feelin O2 Good
10A Flanders Road – **Riverhead**
631-381-0918
www.feelino2good.com

Montauk Salt Cave
552 W. Lake Drive – **Montauk**
631-668-7258
www.montauksaltcave.com

Peconic River Salt
Float, yoga, Reiki
125 E. Main Street – **Riverhead**
631-369-7258
www.peconicsalt.org

HOTELS
B&B's & RESORTS

Amagansett

The Gansett Green Manor
273 Main St
631-267-3133
www.gansettgreenmanor.com

The Hermitage at Napeague
2148 Montauk Hwy
631-267-6151
www.duneresorts.com

Ocean Colony Beach & Tennis Club
2004 Montauk Hwy
631-267-3130
www.duneresorts.com

Ocean Vista Resort
2136 Montauk Hwy
631-267-3448
www.oceanvistaresort.com

Sea Crest on the Ocean
2166 Montauk Hwy
631-267-3159/ 800-SEA DAYS
www.duneresorts.com

Bridgehampton

The Bridge Inn
2668 Montauk Hwy
631-537-2900
www.hamptonsbridgeinn.com

Bridgehampton Inn
2266 Main St
631-537-3660
www.bridgehamptoninn.com

Topping Rose House
1 Bridgehampton-Sag Harbor Turnpike
631-537-0870
www.toppingrosehouse.com

East Hampton

Baker House
181 Main St
631-324-4081
www.bakerhouse1650.com

East Hampton House
226 Pantigo Rd
631-324-4300
www.easthamptonhouseresort.com

East Hampton Point
295 Three Mile Harbor Road
631-324-9191
www.easthamptonpoint.com

Hedges Inn
74 James Lane
631-324-7101
www.thehedgesinn.com

Huntting Inn
94 Main St
631-324-0410
www.hunttinginn.com

The Maindstone
207 Main St
631-324-5006
www.themaidstone.com

Mill House Inn
31 North Main St
631-324-9766
www.millhouseinn.com

1770 House
143 Main St
631-324-1770
www.1770house.com

Montauk

Aquafina Inn
20 S. Elwood Ave
631-668-8300
www.aqualinainmontauk.com

The Atlantic Terrace
21 Oceanview Terrace
631-668-2050
www.atlanticterrace.com

Montauk Hill House
114 Glenmore Ave
631-668-3084
www.montaukhillhouse.com

Montauk Manor
236 Edgemere St.
631-668-4400
www.montaukmanor.com

Montauk Yacht Club Resort
32 Star Island Rd
631-668-3100
www.montaukyachtclub.com

Snug Harbor Motel & Marina
3 Star Island Rd
631-668-2860
www.montauksnugharbor.com

Montauk Blue Hotel
108 S. Emerson Ave
631-668-4000
www.montaukbluehotel.com

Ocean Surf Resort
84 S. Emerson Ave
631-668-3332
www.oceansurfresort.com

The Ocean Resort Inn
95 S. Emerson Ave
631-668-2300
www.oceanresortinn.com

Sole Beach Resort
107 S. Emerson Ave
631-668-6700
www.soleeast.com

Sole East Resort
90 Second House Rd.
631-668-2105
www.soleeast.com

Surf Club at Montauk
20 Surfside Ave
631-668-3800
www.surfclubmontauk.com

Surf Lodge
183 Edgemere St.
631-668-1562
www.surflodge.com

Sag Harbor

American Hotel
49 Main St
631-725-3535
www.theamericanhotel.com

Baron's Cove
31 W. Water St
844-227-6672
www.baronscove.com

Forever Bungalows
765 Rout 114
631-591-0512
www.foreverbungalow.com

Sag Harbor Inn
45 W Water St
631-725-2949
www.sagharborinn.com

Shelter Island

The Chequit
23 Grand Ave
631-749-0018
www.thechequit.com

Dering Harbor Inn
13 Winthrop Rd
631-749- 0900
www.deringharborinn.com

The Pridwin
81 Shore Rd
631-749-0476
www.pridwin.com

Ram's Head Inn
108 S. Ram Island Dr
631-749-0811
www.theramsheadinn.com

Seven on Shelter
7 Stearns Point Rd
631-326-3259
www.sevenonshelter.com

Shelter Island House
11 Stearns Point Rd
631-749-1633
www.shelterislandhouse.com

Sunset Beach Hotel
35 Shore Rd
631-749-2001
www.sunsetbeachli.com

Southampton

A Butler's Manor - The Hamptons B & B
244 N Main St
631-283-8550
www.abutlersmanor.com

The Atlantic
1655 County Rd 39
631-283-6100
www.theatlantichotelsouthampton.com

Capri Hotel Southampton
281 County Rd 39A
631-504-6575
www.caprisouthampton.com

The Easterner Motel
639 Montauk Hwy
631-283-9292
www.easternermotel.com

Hamlet Inn
300 Montauk Hwy
631-283-2968
www.hamletinn.com

Hotel Raphael
29 Woodland Dr
917-991-1077
www.hotelraphael.net

Hotel ZE
136 N. Main St
631-619-6660
www.hotelzesouthampton.us

Latch Pop Up Inn
101 Hill St
631-488-4800
www.latchpopupçom

Southampton Cottages
35 Shrubland Rd
631-287-9600
www.southamptoncottages.com

Southampton Inn
91 Hill St
631-283-6500
www.southamptoninn.com

Southampton Long Island Hotel
450 County Rd 39
631-283-2548
www.hotelofsouthampton.com

Southampton Village Motel
315 Hampton Rd
631-283-3034
www.southamptonvillagemotel.com

White Fences Inn
371 Montauk Hwy
631-500-9013
www.whitefenceswatermill.com

Wainscott

Cozy Cabins Motel
395 Montauk Hwy
631-537-1160
www.thecozycottages.com

Wainscott Inn
3720 Montauk Hwy
631-825-0661
www.wainscottinn.com

380 Inn
380 Montauk Hwy
631-527-7000
www.380inn.com

MUSEUMS & HISTORICAL PLACES

AMAGANSETT

East End Classic Boat Society
301 Bluff Road
631-324-2490
www.eecbs.org

East Hampton Town Marine Museum
301 Bluff Road
631-324-6850
www.easthamptonhistory.org

Miss Amelia's Cottage and Roy Lester Carriage Museum
Main Street
631-267-3020

BRIDGEHAMPTON

Bridgehampton Historical Society
2368 Montauk Hwy
631-537-1088
www.bridgehamptonhistorialsociety.org

South Fork Natural History Museum and Nature Center
377 Bridehampton/Sag Harbor Turnpike - Bridgehampton
631-537-9735
www.sofo.org

EAST HAMPTON

Clinton Academy
51 Main Street
631-324-1850
www.easthamptonhistory.org

East Hampton Village Historical Society
101 Main Street
631-324-6850
www.easthamptonhistory.org

The Leiber Collection
446 Old Stone Highway
631 329-3288
www.leibermuseum.org
Free Admission Memorial Day - Labor Day
Wed., Sat. Sun. 1-4

Osborn-Jackson House
101 Main Street
631-324-6850
www.easthamptonhistory.org

Pollock-Krasner House
830 Springs Fireplace Road
631-324-4929
www.stonybrook.edu/pkhouse

MONTAUK

Montauk Point Lighthouse Museum
Montauk Hwy
631-668-2544
www.montauklighthouse.com

Second House
12 Second House Rd
631-668-5340
www.montauklighthouse.com/second_house.htm

Third House
Montauk Hwy & Theodore Roosevelt County Park
631-852-7878
www.montauklighthouse.com/second_house.htm

SAG HARBOR

Eastville Historical Society
139 Hampton Street
631-725-4711
www.eastvillehistorical.org

Sag Harbor Historical Society
174 Main Street
631-725-5092
www.sagharborhistorical.org

Sag Harbor Whaling Museum
200 Main Street
631-725-0770
www.sagharborwhalingmuseum.org

Whaling Museum
200 Main Street
631-725-0770
www.sagharborwhalingmuseum.org

SOUTHAMPTON

Rogers Mansion
17 Meeting House Ln
631-283-2494
www.southamptonhistoricalmuseum.org

Shinnecock Nation Cultural Center & Museum
100 Montauk Hwy
631-287-4923
www.shinnecockmuseum.com

Southampton Arts Center
25 Job's Lane
631-283-0967
www.southamptoncenter.org

Southampton Cultural Center
25 Pond Lane
631-287-4377
www.scc-arts.org

Southampton Historical Museum
17 Meeting House Lane
631-293-2494
www.southamptonhistoricalmuseum.org

Suffolk County Historical Society
300 West Main Street – Riverhead
631-727-2881
www.suffolkcountyhistoricalsociety.org

WATER MILL

Parrish Art Museum
279 Montauk Hwy
631-283-2118
www.parrishart.org

Water Mill Center
39 Water Mill Towd Road
631-726-4628
www.watermillcenter.org

The Water Mill Museum
41 Old Mill Rd
631-726-4625
www.watermillmuseum.org

PARKS & GARDENS

GARDENS

Bridge Gardens
36 Mitchell Lane - **Bridgehampton**
631-537-7440
www.peconiclandtrust.com

Long House Reserve
133 Hands Creek Road - **East Hampton**
631-329-3568
www.longhouse.org

The Madoo Conservancy
618 Sagg Road - **Sagaponac**k
631-537-8200
www.madoo.org

PARKS & NATURE PRESERVES

Cedar Point County Park
5 Cedar Point Rd – **East Hampton**
631-852-7620
607-acre park with views of Gardiners Bay and a lighthouse
www.suffolkcountyny.gov

East Hampton Nature Trail
Davids Lane – **East Hampton**
Trails, wildlife, parking available

Elizabeth Morton National Wildlife Refuge
748 Noyac Road, - **Sag Harbor**
631-286-0485
187-acre reserve situated on a reserve surrounded by the Noyac & Peconic Bays
www.fws.gov/refuge/elizabeth_a_morton

Group for the East End
2442 Main Street – **Bridgehampton**
www.groupfortheeastend.org

Hither Hills State Park
164 Old Montauk Hwy – **Montauk**
631-668-2554
189-acre campsite on the Atlantic ocean. The "walking dunes" of
Napeague Harbor are located on the eastern side of the park.
www.parks.ny.gov

PETS

ALTERNATIVE MEDICINE & THERAPY

Hampton Veterinary Hospital
176 Montauk Hwy - **Speonk**
631-325-1611
www.hamptonvet.net
Acupuncture and traditional Chinese herbal medicine

Shinnecock Animal Hospital
212 E. Montauk Hwy - **Hampton Bays**
631-887-3501
herbal medicine and acupuncture

Veterinary Acupuncture & Healing Arts
516-242-7209
HOUSE CALLS ONLY FOR: acupuncture, chiropractic, Tui Na massage and Chines herbal medicine.

S.S. Aqua Dog
www.randyproductions.com
Hydrotherapy, Therapeutic Massage, Reiki & Cold Laser Therapy

ANIMAL CONTROL

East Hampton Animal Control
159 Pantigo Road - **East Hampton**
631-324-0085
www.ehamptonny.gov

Shelter Island Animal Control
53 North Ferry Road - **Shelter Island**
631-749-2506
www.CountyOffice.org

Southampton Animal Control
102 Old Riverhead Road - **Hampton Bays**
631-728-1088
www.southamptontownny.gov

ANIMAL RESCUE

Amaryllis Farm Equine Resque
93 Merchants Path - **East Hampton**
631-537-7335
www.amaryllisfarm.com

Animal Rescue Fund of the Hamptons (ARF)
124 Daniels Hole Road - **Wainscott**
631-537-0400
www.arfhamptons.org

Bide – A- Wee
118 Old Country Rd - **Westhampton Beach**
631-325-0280
www.bideawee.org

Elsa's Ark
P.O Box 2900 - **East Hampton**
631-329-2900
www.petfinder.org/shelters

Southampton Animal Rescue
102 Old Riverhead Rd West - **Hampton Bays**
631-728-7387
www.southamptonanimalshelter.com

BOARDING

All Dogged UP
25 W. Neck Road - **Shelter Island Heights**
631-749-0702
www.alldoggedupsi.com

East Hampton Veterinary Group
22 Montauk Hwy - **East Hampton**
631-324-0282
www.easthamptonvetgroup.com

Edge Of Pond Kennels
564 Toppings Path - **Bridgehampton**
631-725-0954

Olde Towne Animal Hospital
380 County Road 39A - **Southampton**
631-283-0611
www.oldetowneanimalhosp.com

South Fork Animal Hospital
340 Montauk Hwy - **Wainscott**
631-537-0035
www.southforkanimalhospital.com

Zen Dog
Settlers Landing Lane - **East Hampton**
631 324-8914
One dog at a time
www.petsittingeasthampton.com

EMERGENCY CENTERS

East End Veterinary Center
67 Commerce Drive – **Riverhead**
24 Hours/7 Days a week
631-369-4513
631-729-8236
www.pet-er.com

Wildlife Rescue Center
**Eastern Long Islands ONLY Wildlife Hospital
228 W. Montauk Hwy - **Hampton Bays**
631-720-4200
www.wildrescuecenter.org

GROOMING

All Dogged Up
25 West Neck Road – **Shelter Island**
631-749-0702
Monday -Friday: 9:00-5:00
Sunday: 11:00-5:00
www.alldoggedupsi.com

Beach Paws, LLC
6 Garbis Lane – **East Hampton**
631-537-4590

Bubbles & Bows Mobile Pet Grooming
For Appointments:
631-533-2697
Bubblesandbows@yahoo.com
www.bubblesandbowsmobile.com

The Classy Canine
468 Country Road 39A – **Southampton**
631-283-1306
www.classycaninehamptons.com

Dapper Dog
42 Snake Hollow Road – **Bridgehampton**
631-537-3355

Happy Tails Mobile Pet Grooming
64 Sunset Lane **– East Hampton**
631-734-2053

Harbor Pets
12 Bay Street – **Sag Harbor**
631-725-9070

Laurens Dog House
141 Springs Fireplace Rd – **East Hampton**
631-204-7517

One Stop Pet Shop
611 Hampton Rd – **Southampton**
631-287-6001
www.1stoppetshops.com

Shinnecock Animal Hospital
212 E. Montauk Hwy **– Hampton Bays**
631-887-3501
www.sahospital@optonline.net

Westhampton Dog Grooming
70 Oak Street – **Westhampton**
631-288-3678

Westhampton Pets
60 Old Riverhead Road - **Westhampton**
631-288-6765
www.westhamptonpets.net

OBEDIENCE TRAINING

ARF Dog Training Classes
124 Daniels Hole Road - **Wainscott**
631-537-0400
www.arfhamptons.org

Gebbia Dan Professional Dog Trainer
1065 Majors Path - **Southampton**
631-287-4460
www.dangebbiadogtrainer.com

Lisa Hartman
786-942-7387
www.lisathedogtrainer.com

Nikki Wood
631-903-7210
www.hamptonsdogtraining.com

PET SITTING & WALKING

All Dogged Up
25 West Neck Road – **Shelter Island**
631-749-0702
www.alldoggedupsi.com

Bark Canine Care
631-707-5337
nannoeli@optonline.net
Boarding, beach runs, home visits, elder care

Fuzzy Friends Foundation
631-702-0882
Fuzzyfriendsfoundation@hotmail.com
In home pet care, drop off and pickup service, daily walks and feelings

Happy Hound Daily Dog Services
631-764-9295 - Abby
Walking – private and group walks – beach and trail adventures, mid-day potty breaks, pet taxi

Lori's Full-Service Pet Care
10 Saddle Lane – **East Hampton**
631-697-3558
www.lorisfullservicepetcare.com
Dog Walking & Adventure, House Visits, Overnights

Montauk Pet Sitters
631-668-2195

Pampered Paws
Springs Fireplace Road – **East Hampton**
631-655-5812
www.pamperedpawseh@gmail.com
Sitting, walking, grooming

Pet Sitting Service by Chris -Dogs & Cats
516-641-1660
Walking, kitty care, vet visits

Pet Sitting Perfected
105 Oak View Highway – **East Hampton**
631-371-7274
www.petsittingperfected.com

Sag Harbor Pet Sitting
631-702-3539
www.sagharborpetsitting.com

PET FRIENDLY HOTELS
Amagansett

Gansett Green Manor
273 Main Street
631-267-3133
www.gansettgreenmanor.com
Pet Fee: $25/night

Bridgehampton

Topping Rose House
1 Bridgehampton Sag Harbor Turnpike
631-537-0870
www.toppingrosehouse.com
Pet Fee: $35/pets up to 35lbs

East Hampton

The Maidstone
207 Main Street
631-324-5006
www.themaidstone.com
Pet Fee: 2 pets – any size – No pet fee

Mill House Inn
31 N. Main Street
631-324-9766
www.millhouseinn.com
Pet Fee : $60/night/dog

Montauk

Daunts Albatross Motel
44 S. Elmwood Ave
631-668-2729
www.dauntsalbatross.com
Pet Fee: $25/night/some rooms

Kenny's Tipperary Inn
432 West Lake Drive
631-668-2010
www.thetipperaryinn.com
Pet Fee: $50 off season/ $125 Summer – entire stay

Snug Harbor Motel & Marina
3 Star Island Road
631-668-2860
www.montauksnugharbor.com
Pet Fee: $30/night

Sole East Beach
90 Second House Road
631-668-2105
www.soleeast.com
Pet Fee : $200 entire stay/ some rooms

Shelter Island

Shelter Island House
11 Sterns Point Rd
631-749-1633
www.shelterislandhouse.com
Pet Fee: $150 - 50lbs and under

Sag Harbor

Barons Cove
31 W. Water Street
844-227-6672
www.baronscove.com
Pet Fee : $100/night – 50lbs and under

Southampton

The Atlantic
1655 County Road 39
631-283-6100
www.atlantichotelsouthampton.com
Pet Fee: $40/night/pet -2 pets up to 40lbs

Capri
281 County 39A
631-504-6575
www.caprisouthampton.com
Pet Fee: $40/night/pet

Southampton Inn
91 Hill Street
631-283-6500
www.southamptoninn.com
Pet Fee: $49/night/per – 2 pets maximum

PET SUPPLY STORES

Agway
125 Snake Hollow Rd - Bridgehampton
631-537-0007
www.agwaycountrygardens.com

Harbor Pets
12 Bay Street - Sag Harbor
631-725-9070
www.sagharborpetsitting.com

Montauk Plaza Pet Supplies
7 The Plaza - Montauk
631-668-3785

One Stop Pet
136 Main Street - Amagansett
631-267-7535
AND:
20 Hampton Road - Southampton
631-287-6001
www.1stoppetshops.com

Petco Animal Supplies
2044 Montauk Hwy, Ste 24 - Bridgehampton Commons
631-537-1853
www.stores.petco.com

Reptile Bob's Ponds & Pets
2 Carter Lane - East Quogue
631-653-3300
www.reptilebobs.com

Westhampton Pets
60 Old Riverhead Road - Westhampton Beach
631-277-6765
www.westhamptonpet.net

VETERINARIANS
East Hampton

EAST HAMPTON VETERINARY GROUP
22 Montauk Highway
631-722-7171
Monday – Saturday: 8:00-5:00
Sunday: 9:30-1:00
www.easthamptonvetgroup.com

VETERINARY CLINIC OF EAST HAMPTON
3 Goodfriend Drive
631-324-7900
Monday, Thursday, Friday: 9:00-5:00
Tuesday, Wednesday: 9:00-8:00
Saturday, Sunday: 9:00-4:00

Sag Harbor

SAG HARBOR VETERINARY CLINIC
28 Bridge Street
631-725-6500
www.sagharborvet.com

Shelter Island

NORTH FORK ANIMAL HOSPITAL
53 North Ferry Road
631-749-2506
Mon,Wed,Thurs,Fri,Sat: 10:00-1:00
Tuesday: 10:00-5:00
Sunday: Closed
www.northforkanimalhospital.com

Southampton & Vicinity

ANIMAL CLINIC OF HAMPTON BAYS
238 W. Montauk Hwy – **Hampton Bays**
631-728-0800
Monday – Friday: 8:30-6:00
Saturday: 8:30-3:00
www.animalclinicofhamptonbays.com

NORTH FORK ANIMAL HOSPITAL
58605 Rout 25 – **Southold**
631-765-2400
Monday – Thursday: 8:00-7:00
Friday-Saturday: 8:00-5:00
Sunday: 8:00-10:00

OLDE TOWNE ANIMAL HOSPITAL
380 County Road 39A - **Southampton**
631-283-0611
Monday-Friday: 8:00-6:00
Saturday: 8:00-5:00
Sunday: 10:00-5:00
www.OldeTowneAH@optonline.net

PECONIC BAY ANIMAL HOSPITAL
1149 Old Country Road **– Riverhead**
631-740-9282
Mon,Wed,Fri: 9:00-5:00
www.peconicpet.com

SHINNECOCK ANIMAL HOSPITAL
212 East Montauk Hwy - **Hampton Bays**
631-887-3501
Monday, Wednesday, Friday: 9:00-6:00
Tuesday, Thursday: 9:00-8:00
Saturday: 9:00-4:00
www.sahospital.net

WESTHAMPTON BEACH ANIMAL HOSPITAL
126 Montauk Hwy - **Westhampton Beach**
631-625-4031
Monday, Wednesday: 8:00-8:00
Tuesday, Thursday, Friday: 8:00-6:00
Saturday, Sunday: 9:00-4:00

Wainscott

SOUTHFORK ANIMAL HOSPITAL
340 Montauk Hwy
631-537-0035
Monday – Friday: 8:00-5:00
Saturday: 8:00-3:00
Sunday: Closed
www.southforkanimalhospital.com

HOUSE CALLS:

DR. CINDY BRESSLER
631-255-8556
www.drcindybressler.com
**Hamptons Canine Concierge- a luxury service providing accom-
modations, drivers, private jets, event planning, play dates, swimming lessons, training, grooming and spa.

DR. NORA KLEPS
516-449-1339
www.norakleps.com
**mobile clinic AKA : HOOVES, PAWS AND CLAWS

DR. ANDREW PEPPER
631-449-7829
www.pepmobilevet.com

PLACES OF WORSHIP

Amagansett

First Presbyterian Church of Amagansett
350 Main Street
631-267-6404
Services: Sunday   11:00 a.m.
www.amagansettpresbyterian.org

St. Michael's Lutheran Church
287 Montauk Hwy
631-267-6351
Services: Sunday   11:00 a.m
www.hamptonslutheran.org

St. Peter's The Apostle Catholic Church
286 Main Street
631-324-0134
Services: Sunday   9:00 Summer Only
www.mht-eh.org

St. Thomas Episcopal Church
Indian Wells Highway and Montauk Highway
313-242-7356
www.episcopalchurch.org/parish/st-thomas-episcopal-chapel-amagansett-ny

Bridgehampton

Bridgehampton Presbyterian Church
2429 Montauk Hwy
631-537-0863
Services: Sunday   10:30 a.m.
www.bridgehamptonpc.org

Bridgehampton United Methodist
Corner of Church Street & Montauk Hwy
631-537-0753
Services: Sunday   11:00 a.m.

First Baptist Church of Bridgehampton
141 Bridgehampton/Sag Harbor Turnpike
631-537-0288
Services: Sunday   11:00 a.m
July/August: Sunday   10:00 a.m.
www.1stbaptistchurchbh.org

Incarnation Lutheran ELCA
59 Hayground Road
631-537-1187
Services: Sunday   9:00 a.m.

Queen of the Most Holy Rosary
2350 Montauk Hwy
631-537-0156
Services: Monday-Thursday   7:30 a.m.
               Saturday   5:00 p.m.
               Sunday   10:00 a.m. ENGLISH
               Sunday   11:30 a.m. Espanol
www.qmhr.org

St. Ann's Episcopal Church
2463 Main Street
631-537-1527
Services: Sunday   9:30 a.m
www.stannsbh.org

Unitarian Universalist Congregation of the South Fork
977 Bridgehampton-Sag Harbor Turnpike
631-537-0132
Services: Sunday   10:30 a.m.
www.uucsf.org

East Hampton

Calvary Baptist Church
60 Spinner Lane
631-324-5313
Services: Sunday   10:45 a.m & 6:30 p.m.
www.cbceasthampton.com

Church of Christ
500 Sag Harbor Turnpike
631-749-0090

First Presbyterian of East Hampton
120 Main Street
631-324-0711
Services: Sunday   10:00 a.m.
www.fpceh.org

United Methodist Church of East Hampton
35 Pantigo Road
631-324-4258
www.umc.org

Jewish Center of the Hamptons
44 Woods Lane
631-324-9858
www.jcoh.org

Most Holy Trinity RC Church
57 Buell Lane
631-324-0134
Services: Sunday   9:30 & 11:30 a.m.
En Espanol   Sunday   7:00 p.m.

Springs Community Presbyterian
5 Springs Fireplace Road
631-324-4791

St. Luke's Episcopal Church
18 James Lane
631-329-0990
Services: Sunday   8:00 & 10:00 a.m.
www.stlukeseasthampton.org

St. Peter's Chapel Springs
463 Old Stone Highway
631-329-6465
Services: Saturday   5:30 p.m.

Montauk

Montauk Community Church
850 Montauk Hwy
631-669-2022
Services: Sunday   10:00 a.m.
www.montaukcommunitychurch.org

St. Therese of Lisieux RC
68 S. Essex Street
631-668-2200
Services:

First Friday	8:30 a.m.	
Saturday	5:00 p.m. & 8:00 p.m. (Spanish)	
Sunday	8:30 a.m. & 10:30 a.m.	

Shelter Island

Grace Evangelical Church
44 South Ferry Rd
631-749-6169

Our Lady of the Isle Roman Catholic Church
7 Prospect Ave
631-749-0001
www.ourladyoftheisle.org

Shelter Island Presbyterian Church
32 North Ferry Rd
631-749-0805
Services: Sunday   10:30 a.m.
www.sipchurch.org

St. Mary's Episcopal Church
26 Saint Mary's Rd
631-749-0770
Services: Sunday   8:00 a.m. & 10:00 a.m.
www.stmarysshelterisland.org

Sag Harbor

Christ Episcopal Church
5 Hampton Street
631-725-0128
Services: Sunday   8:00 & 10:00 a.m.
www.christchurchshny.org

Community Bible Church
2837 Noyac road
631-725-4155
Services: Sunday   10:00 a.m.
www.cbchamptons.com

Old Whalers Church
44 Union Street
631-725-0894
Services: Sunday   10:00 a.m.
www.oldwhalerschurch.org

St. Andrew RC Church
122 Division Street
631-725-0123
Services:

Monday-Friday	9:00 a.m.
Saturday	9:00 a.m. & 5:00 p.m.
Sunday	8:30 a.m., 10:00 a.m. & 11:30 a.m.

Temple Adas Israel
30 Atlantic Ave
631-725-0904
www.templeadasisrael.org

Southampton

Community Baptist Church
16 Reverend Raymond Lee Court
631-283-8332

First Baptist Church
57 Halsey Avenue
631-283-4651

First Church of Christian Scientist
70 Cameron Street
631-283-5772
Services: Sunday   10:30 a.m.
www.christiansciencehamptons.org

First Presbyterian of Southampton
2 South Main Street
631-283-1296
Services: Sunday   10:00 a.m.
www.1stpresbyterian.church

Greek Orthodox Church of the Hamptons
111 Saint Andrews Circle
631-283-6169
Services: Sunday   10:00 a.m.
www.kimisishamptons.org

Our Lady of Poland RC
35 Maple Street
631-283-0667
Services:

Weekdays	7:30 a.m.
Sunday	6:30, 9:30 & 11:45 a.m.
	8:00 & 10:30 a.m. (Polish)

Sacred Hearts of Jesus and Mary
168 Hill Street
631-283-0097
Services:

Mon,Wed,Thurs,Fri	12:00 p.m.
Tuesday	8:00 a.m.
Saturday	5:00 p.m.
Sunday	8:00, 9:30 & 11:00 a.m
	12:30 (Spanish)
	5:00 p.m.

www.shjmbasilica.org

St. John's Episcopal Church
100 S. Main Street
631-283-0549
Services:

Monday – Friday	7:50 a.m. & 5:10 p.m.
Wednesday	10:00 a.m.
Sunday	8:00, 9:00 & 11:00 a.m.

Southampton Full Gospel
130 County Road 39A
631-283-6829
www.missionreachout.org

Hamptons United Methodist
160 Main Street
631-283-0951
Services: Sunday   10:30 a.m.
www.hamptonsumc.org

Wainscott

Living Water Full Gospel Church
69 Industrial Road
631-537-2120
Services: Sunday   8:45 & 10:15 a.m.
www.lwfgc.or

Water Mill

Grace Presbyterian Church
1225 Montauk Hwy
631-726-6100
Services: Sunday   10:00 a.m.
www.gracehamptons.org

Kingdom Hall of Jehovahs Witnesses
38 Scuttle Hole Rd
631-537-0504
Services: Sunday

RESTAURANTS

Amagansett

Astro's Pizza
*Italian
237 Main Street
621-267-8300
www. astropizza.com

Best Taste Restaurant
*Chinese
724 Montauk Highway
631-267-8801
www.newbesttaste.com

Clam Bar
*Seafood
2025 Montauk Highway
631-267-6348
www.clambaronline.com

Hampton Chutney
*South Indian
12 Amagansett Square
631-267-3131
www.hamptonchutney.com

Indian Wells Tavern
*Pub
177 Main Street
631-267-0400
www.indianwellstavern.com

La Fondita
*Southwest Mexican
74 Montauk Hwy
631-267-8800
www.lafondita.net

The Lobster Roll
*Seafood
1980 Montauk Highway
631-267-3740
www.lobsterroll.com

Organic Crush
*Vegan, Vegetarian, Juice
207 Main Street
631-527-7717
www.organickrush.com

Sotto Sopra
*Italian
231 Main Street
631-267-3695
www.restaurantsottosopra.com

The Squeezery
*Juice Bar, Smoothies, Salads
195 Main Street
www.thesqueezery.com

Wolffer Kitchen
*American
4 Amagansett Square Drive
631-267-2764
www.amagansett.wolfferkitchen.com

Zakura
*Sushi, seafood
40 Montauk Highway
631-267-7600
www.zakurasushi.com

Bridgehampton

Almond
*Casual American French
1 Ocean Road
631-537-5665
www.almondrestaurant.com

Bobby Van's Steakhouse
*American
2393 Main Street
631-537-0590
www.bobbyvans.com

Bridgehampton Inn
*American
2266 Montauk Hwy
631-537-3660
www.bridgehamptoninn.com

Candy Kitchen Ice Cream Parlor & Eatery
*Diner, Classic Soda fountain
Montauk Hwy
631-537-9885
www.candykitchen.com

Elaia Estiatorio
*Greek, Mediterranean
95 School Street
631-613-6469
www.esaiaestiatorio.com

Fairway Restaurant – Poxabogue Golf Course
*Breakfast & Brunch, American
3556 Montauk Hwy
631-537-7195

Golden Pear
Casual Cafe
2426 Montauk Highway
631-537-1100
www.goldenpearcafe.com

Mercado Mexican Grill
*Modern Mexican
1970 Montauk Hwy
631-237-1334
www.mercadony.com

Panera Bread
*Bakery, Deli, Salads
2044 Montauk Hwy-Bridgehampton Commons
631-537-2855

Pierre's
*French
2468 Main Street
631-537-5110
www.pierresbridgehampton.com

Salt Drift Farm Eatery
*Farm to Table
203 Bridgehampton Sag Harbor Turnpike
631-488-0581
www.hamptonsaristocrat.com

Topping Rose House
*American
1 Bridgehampton- Sag Harbor Turnpike
631-587-0870
www.toppingrosehouse.com

World Pie
*American, Brick Oven Pizza, Seasonal
2402 Montauk Highway
631-537-7999
www.worldpiebh.com

Yama Q
*Japanese, Seafood, Sushi,Vegetarian
2393 Montauk Hwy
631-537-0225
www.yamaq.com

East Hampton

Babette's
*Seafood, Vegan
66 Newtown Lane
631-329-5377
www.babetteseasthampton.com

Bay Kitchen Bar
*Seafood, American
39 Gann Road
631-329-3663
www.baykitchenbar.com

The Blend
*Northern Italian
367 Three Mile Harbor Road
631-527-7753
www.theblendatthreemileharbor.com

Blue Parrot Bar & Grill
*Mexican
33A Main Street
631-329-2583
www.blueparroteasthampton.com

Bostwick's Chowder House
*Seafood
277 Pantigo Road
631-324-1111
www.bostwickschowderhouse.com

Chen's Garden
*Chinese
478 Pantingo Road
631-329-3232
www.chensgardeneasthampton.com

Cittanuova
*Northern Italian
29 Newtown Lane
631-324-6300
www.cittanuova.com

Cove Hollow Tavern
*American
85 Montauk Highway
631-527-7131
www.covehollowtavern.com

Dopo La Spiaggia
*Italian
31 Race Lane
631-658-9063
www.dopolaspiaggia.com

East Hampton Grill
*Contemporary American
99 N. Main Street
631-329-6666
www.easthamptongrill.com

EMP Summer House
*American
341 Pantigo Road
631-324-3444
www.empsummerhouse.com

Fierros Pizza
*Pizza
104 Park Place
631-324-5751

Fresno
*New American
8 Fresno Place
631-324-8700
www.fresnorestaurant.com

Fusion Express
*Chinese
66 Newtown Lane
631-324-1999

Golden Pear
*Cafe
34 Newtown Lane
631-324-1600

Harbor Bistro
*Seafood, American
313 Three Mile Harbor Road
631-324-7300
www.harborbistro.net

Harbor East
*New American
44 Three Mile Harbor Rd
631-408-5771
www.harboreasthampton.com

John Papas Cafe
*Diner, American Traditional
18 Park Place
631-324-5400
www.johnpapscafe.com

The Living Room
*Scandinavian
207 Main Street
631-324-5006
www.themaidstone.com

Michael's at Maidstone Beach
*Seafood, Steakhouse
28 Maidstone Park Road
631-324-0725
www.michaelsofmaidstone.com

Moby's
*Coastal Italian
295 Three Mile Harbor Road
(Unavailable at time of publication)
www.mobys.com

Nick & Toni's
*Italian
136 N. Main Street
631-324-3550
www.nickandtonis.com

The Palm
*Steakhouse, American
94 Main Street
631-324-0411
www.thepalm.com

Rowdy Hall
*Pub
10 Main Street
631-324-8555
www.rowdyhall.com

Sam's
*Italian, Pizza
36 Newtown Lane
631-324-5900
www.samseasthampton.com

Serafina
*Italian
104 N. Main Street
631-267-3500
www.serafinarestaurant.com

Simply Sublime
*Vegan, Vegetarian
85 Springs Fireplace Road
631-604-1566
www.simplysublimehamptons.com

Smokin' Wolf
*Barbeque
221 Pantigo Road
631-329-7166

Springs Tavern
*Gastro Pub
15 Fort Pond Blvd.
631-527-7800
www.thespringstavern.com

Zok-Kon
*Japanese-Asian
47 Montauk Highway
631-604-5585

1770 House Restaurant
*American
143 Main Street
631-324-1770
www.1770house.com

Montauk

Anthony's Pancake House
*Pancakes, Breakfast
710 Montauk Hwy
631-668-9705

Arbor
*Mediterranean
240 Fort Pond Blvd
631-238-5430
www.arbormontauk.com

Backyard @ Sole East
*Mediterranean
90 Second House Road
631-668-9739
www.soleeast.com/restaurant

Bliss Kitchen
*Coffee, breakfast, sandwiches
732 Montauk Highway
631-668-8206
www.blissmtk.com

Clam & Chowderhouse at Salivars Dock
*Seafood
470 W Lake Drive
631-668-6252
www.clamandchowderhouse.com

Craft Burger
*Burgers, Breakfast, Brunch
440 West Lake Drive
631-438-5959

The Crows Nest
* Mediteranean & Seafood
4 Old West Lake Drive
631-688-2077
www.crowsnestinn.com

Dave's Gone Fishing
*Seafood
467 E. Lake Drive
631-668-9190
www.davesgonefishing.com

The Dock
*Seafood
482 W. Lake Drive
631-668-9778
www.thedockmontauk.com

Duryea's Lobster Deck
*Seafood
65 Tuthill Road
631-668-2410
www.duryealobsters.com

East By Northeast
*Seafood
51 S. Edgemere Street
631-668-2872
www.eastbynortheast.com

Fishbar
*Seafood
467 E. Lake Drive
631-668-6600
www.freshlocalfish.com

Flagship
*Seafood
466 W. Lake Drive
631-668-8260
www.flagshipmontauk.com

668 Gig Shack
*Seafood
782 Main Street
631-668-2727
www.668thegigshack.com

Gosman's Dock
*Seafood
500 W. Lake Drive
631-668-5330
www.gosmans.com

Grey Lady
*Seafood
440 West Lake Drive
631-210-6249
www.greyladymtk.com

Gringos Burrito Grill
*Mexican
805 Main Street
631-668-7500
www.gringosburritogrillmtk.com

Gulf Coast Kitchen
* Fusion
32 Star Island Road
631-668-3100
www.montaukyachtclub.com

Harvest on Fort Pond
* American & Seafood
11 S. Emery Street
631-668-5574
www.harvest2000.com

Hoodoos MTK
*Sandwiches, Breakfast, Brunch
38 S Etna Ave
631-238-5791
www.hoodoosmtk.com

130

Inlet Seafood
*Seafood
541 E. Lake Drive
631-668-4272
www.inletseafood.com

Johns Drive-In
*Burgers, American
677 Main Street
631-668-5518

Joni's Kitchen
* Cafe, Breakfast & Lunch
28 S. Etna Ave
631-668-3663
www.jonismontauk.com

Montauket
*American
88 Firestone Road
631-668-5992
www.montauksun.com

Montauk Lobster House
*Seafood
716 Montauk Highway
New to Montauk. No info at time of print

Montauk Yacht Club
Seafood
32 Star Island Road
631-668-3100
www.montaukyachtclub.com

Muse at the End
*New American
41 S. Euclid Ave
631-238-5937
www.museattheend.com

Navy Beach
*Seafood & Burgers
16 Navy Road
631-668-6868
www.navybeach.com

O'Murphy's
* Irish/ American Pub
432 W. Lake Drive
631-668-50005
www.omurphsrestaurant.com

Pizza Village
* Pizza
700 Montauk Highway
631-778-2232

Quinchos
* Latin American
10 S Etna Ave
631-438-5858

Ricks Crabby Cowboy
* Seafood
435 E Lake Drive
631-668-3200
www.crabbycowboy.com

Ruschmeyers Restaurant
* American
161 Second House Road
631-668-2877

Saltbox
*American
99 Carl Fisher Plaza
631-238-5727
www.montauksaltbox.com

Sammy's
*Seafood
448 West Lake Drive
631-238-5707

Scarpetta Beach @ Gurney's
*Italian
260 Old Montauk Hwy
631-668-2345
www.scarpettarestaurants.com

Shagwong
*Seafood
774 Main Street
631-668-3050

South Edison
*Seafood
17 S. Edison Drive
631-668-4200
www.southedison.com

The Surfside Inn
*American, Seafood
685 Old Montauk Hwy
631-668-5958
www.surfsideinnmontauk.com

Surf Lodge
*Seafood
183 Edgemere Street
631-668-1562
www.thesurflodge.com

Swallow East
*New American
474 West Lake Drive
631-668-8344
www.swalloweastrestaurant.com

Tauk at Trails End
*Seafood
63 S. Euclid Ave.
631 238-5527
www.taukattrailsend.com

Tre Bella Italian Restaurant
*Italian
236 Edgemere St – Montauk Manor
631-668-2322
www.trebellarestaurant.com

West Lake Clam & Chowder House
*Seafood
382 W. Lake Drive
631-668-6252

Sag Harbor

The American Hotel
*American
49 Main Street
631-725-3535
www.theamericanhotel.com

Barons Cove
*American
31 W. Water Street
844-227-6672
www.baronscove.com

Bagel Buoy
* Bagels, Sandwiches
3 Bay Street
631-725-7690
www.bagelbuoy.com

Bay Burger
*Burgers
1742 Bridgehampton Sag Harbor Turnpike
631-899-3914
www.bayburger.com

Beacon
*New American
8 W. Water Street
631-725-7088
www.beaconsagharbor.com

Bell & Anchor
*Seafood
3253 Noyac Road
631-725-3400
www.bellandanchor.com

Corner Bar
*Burgers/ American
1 Main Street
631-725-97605
www.cornerbarsagharbor.com

The Dock House
*Seafood
1 Long Wharf
631-725-7555
www.dockhouse.com

Dockside Bar & Grill
*Seafood
26 Bay Street
631-725-7100
www.docksidesagharbor.com

Dopo La Spiaggia
*Italian
6 Bay Street
631-725-7009
www.dopolaspiaggia.com

Espresso's Da Asport
Italian Comfort Food, Sandwiches take out
2 Main Street
631-725-5668
www.espressodaasporta.com

Estia's Little Kitchen
*American
1615 Bridgehampton – Sag Harbor Turnpike
631-725-1045
www.estias.com

IL Capuccino Ristorante
* Italian
30 Madison Street
631-725-2747
www.ilcapuccino.com

Le Bilboquet
*French Bistro
1 Long Wharf
631-808-3767
www.lebilboquetny.com

LT Burger
*Burgers, Salads
62 Main Street
631-899-4646
www.ltburger.com

Lulu Kitchen & Bar
*New American
126 Main Street
631-725-0900
www.lulusagharbor.com

M.J. Dowlings Steakhouse & Bar
*Steakhouse
3360 Noyac Road
631-725-4444
www.mjdowlings.com

Page at 63 Main
*American
63 Main Street
631-725-1810
www.page63main.com

Sen
*Sushi
23 Main Street
631-725-1774
www.senrestaurant.com

Sing City
* Dim Sum
22 Long Island Ave
631-725-9888

Tutto Il Giorno
*Southern Italian
16 Main Street
www.tuttoilgiorno.com

Wolffer Kitchen
*American
29 Main Street
631-725-0101
www.wolfferkitchen.com

Shelter Island

18 Bay Restaurant
*Italian
23 N. Ferry Rd
631-749-0053
www.18bayrestaurant.com

Cafe 27
*Breakfast, Cafe
27 N. Ferry Rd
631-749-2727

Commander Cody's Seafood
*Seafood
41 Smith St
631-749-1851

The Dory
*American
185 N. Ferry Rd
631-749-4300

Mamas Kitchen
*Mexican
55 N. Ferry Rd
631-749-5450

The Pridwin
*New American
81 Shore Rd
631-749-0476
www.pridwin.com

Rams Head Inn
*American
108 Ram Island Rd
631-749-0811
www.theramsheadinn.com

Salt
*Seafood, American
63 S. Menantic
631-749-5535
www.saltshelterisland.com

Stars Cafe
*Tex Mex
17 Grand Ave
631-749-5345
www.starscafeshelterisland.com

Sunset Beach
* Seafood
35 Shore Road
631-749-2001
www.sunsetbeachli.com

The Tavern at Shelter Island House
*American, Grill, Seafood
11 Stearns Point Rd
631-749-5659
www.shelterislandhouse.com

Vine Street Cafe
*American
41 S. Ferry Road
631-749-3210
www.vinestreefcafe.com

Southampton

75 Main
*American
75 Main Street
631-283-7575
www.75main.com

Boa Thai Asian Fusion
*Asian Fusion
129 Noyac Road
631-488-4422
www.boathai.com

China Garden
* Chinese
26 Hampton Road
631-283-8812

The Coast Grill
*Seafood & American
1109 Noyac Road
631-283-2277
www.thecoastgrillrestaurant.com

Dragon Garden
* Chinese
369 N. Sea Road
631-283-7703
www.chinesetakeoutsouthamptonny.com

Fellinghams Sports Bar
*Burgers, Salads
17 Cameron Street
631-283-9417
www.fellinghamsrestaurant.com

Four Oaks Cafe
*Café, Juice bar, Smoothies, Vegetarian & Vegan
42 Jagger Lane
631-287-6445

Golden Pear
*Café Coffee Shop
99 Main Street
631-283-8900
www.goldenpear.com

Hampton Coffee Company
* Café
749 County Road 39A
631-353-3088
www.hamptoncoffeecompany.com

Jobs Lane Gastro Pub
*Gastropub, Salad, Burger
10 Windmill Lane
631-287-8703
www.jobslanegastropub.com

La Enramada
*Latin American
450 County Road 39
631-259-8999

La Hacienda
*Mexican
48 Jagger Lane
631-287-6814

La Parmigiana Italian Restaurant
*Pizza, Italina
48 Hampton Road
731-283-8030
 www.laparmigianaitalianrestaurant.com

Le Charlot
*French
36 Main Street
631-353-3222
www.le.charlotsouthampton.com

Little Red
*French Inspired American
76C Jobs Lane
631-283-3300
www.littleredsouthampton.com

Mount Fuji
*Japanese & Sushi
1670 County Road 39
631-287-1700
www.mtfujisouthampton.com

Oreya
*French American
281 County Road 39A
631-500-9055
www.oreyahamptons.com

Paul's Italian
*Pizza & Italian
21 Hill St
631-283-1861
www.paulsitalianrestaurant.com

Pellegrino's
* Italian & Pizza Bar
1271 Noyac Road
631-283-9742
www.pellegrinospizzabar.com

Plaza Cafe
*Seafood
61 Hill Street
631-283-9323
www.plazacafe.us

Red Bar Brasserie
*International
210 Hampton Road
631-283-0704
www.redbarbrasserie.com

Saaz Indian Cuisine
*Indian
1746 County Road 39
631-259-2222
www.saazindian.com

Sant Ambroeus
*Italian, European
30 N. Main Street
631-283-1233
www.santambroeus.com

Shippy's Restaurant
*German
36 Windmill Lane
631-283-0007
www.shippyspumpernickels.com

Silver's
*New American, French
15 Main Street
631-283-6443
www.silversrestaurant.com

Sip N Soda Luncheonette
*American
40 Hampton Road
631-283-9752
www.sipnsode.com

Southampton Public House
*American, Brewery
62 Jobs Lane
631-283-2800
www.publick.com

Southampton Social Club
*Sushi & Seafood
256 Elm St
631-287-1400
www.southamptonsocialclub.com

Tutto il Giorno South
*Italian
56 Nugent Street
631-377-361
 www.tuttiolgiorno.com

Union Cantina
*Mexican Farm to Table
40 Bowden Square
631-377-3500
www.unioncantina.com

Wainscott

Highway Restaurant & Bar
*New American
290 Montauk Hwy
631-527-5372
 www.highwayrestaurant.com

Il Mulino
*Italian
108 Wainscott Stone Road
www.ilmulino.com

La Capannina
*Italian, Pizza
364 Montauk Hwy
631-569-4524
www.lacapanninapizza.com

Old Stove Pub
*Greek
3516 Montauk Hwy
631-537-3300

Phoenix
*Chinese
352 Montauk Hwy
631-537-0011
www.phoenixwainscott.com

Town Line BBQ
*BBQ
3593 Montauk Hwy
631-537-2271
www.townlinebbq.com

Water Mill

Calissa
*Mediterranean, Greek
1020 Montauk Highway
631-500-9292
www.calissahamptons.com

Bistro Ete
*Contemporary French
760 Montauk Hwy
631-500-9085
www.bistroete.com

Hampton Coffee Company
* Café
869 Montauk Highway
631-726-2633
www.hamptoncoffeecompany.com

Manna Restaurant
*Modern European
670 Montauk Hwy
631-726-4444
www.mannahamptons.com

Sabrosa Mexican Grill
*Healthy Mexican
1152 Montauk Hwy
631-723-6565
www.sambrosamexicangrill.com

Suki Zuki
*Japanese
688 Montauk Highway
631-726-4600

Wangs No.1 Chinese Restaurant
* Chinese
670 Montauk Highway
631-726-8080

RESTAURANTS WITH SUNSET VIEWS

East Hampton

Bay Kitchen Bar
39 Gann Road
631-329-3663
www. Baykitchenbar.com

Harbor Bistro
313 Three Mile Hog Creek Road
631-324-7300
www.harborbistro.net

Moby's
*Coastal Italian
295 Three Mile Harbor Road
(Unavailable at time of publication)
www.mobys.com

Montauk

Crow's Nest Inn
4 Old West Lake Drive
631-668-2077
www.crowsnestmtk.com

Duryea's Lobster Deck
65 Tuthill Road
631-668-2410
www.duryealobsters.com

East by Northeast
51 Edgemere Street
631-668-2872
www.eastbynortheast.com

The Harvest on Fort Pond
11 S. Emery Street
631-668-5574
www.harvestfortpond.com

The Montauket
88 Firestone Rd
631- 668-5992
www.montauksun.com

Montauk Yacht Club
32 Star Island Road
631-668-3100
www.montaukyachtclub.com

Scarpetta Beach
290 Old Montauk Hwy
631-668-2345
www.gurneysmontauk.com

Surf Lodge
183 Edgemere Street
631-483-5037
www.surflodge.com

Sag Harbor

Barons Cove
31 West Water Street
844-227-6672
www.baronscove.com

The Beacon
 8 West Water Street
631-725-7088
www.beaconsagharbor.com

Shelter Island

Sunset Beach
35 Shore Road
631-749-2001
www.sunsetbeachli.com

Pridwin Hotel Restaurant
81 Shore Road
631-749-0476
www.pridwin.com

Southampton

Coast Grill
1109 Noyac Road
631-283-2277
www.thecoastgrillrestaurant.com

SPORTS & RECREATION

BIKE RENTALS

Amagansett Beach & Bicycle Company
624 Montauk Hwy - Amagansett
888-494-6167
www.amagansettbeachco.com

Bermuda Bikes
36 Gingerbread Lane - East Hampton
631-324-6688
www.bermudabikes.com

Khanh Sports
60 Park Place - East Hampton
631-324-0703
www.khanhsports.com

Khanh Sports
500 Montauk Highway – Amagansett
631-324-1077

Montauk Bike Shop
725 Montauk Hwy - Montauk
631-668-8975
www.montaukbikeshop.com

Piccozzi's Bike Shop
177 N. Ferry Road – Shelter Island
631-749-0045

Rotations Bicycle Center
32 Windmill Lane - Southampton
631-238-2890
www.rotationsbicyclecenter.com

Sag Harbor Cycle Company
34 Bay Street - Sag Harbor
631-725-1110
www.sagharborcycle.com

SKY SPORTS

FLYING:
Sound Aircraft Flight Enterprises
200 Daniels Hole Rd - Wainscott
631-537-2202
www.soundaircraft.com

GLIDING:
Sky Sailors Glider School
313 Francis S. Gabreski Airport - Westhampton
631-288-5858

SKYDIVING:
Skydive Long Island
135 Dawn Drive - Shirley
631-208-3900
www.longislandskydiving.com

GOLF COURSES - PUBLIC

Bethpage State Park Golf Courses
99 Quaker Meetinghouse Road - Farmingdale
631-283-1389

Montauk Downs
S. Fairview Avenue - Montauk
631-668-5000
www.parks.ny.gov/golf-courses

Poxabogue Golf Center
Montauk Hwy - Bridgehampton
631-537-0025
www.poxgolf.com

Sag Harbor
Barcelona Pt. Road - Sag Harbor
631-725-2503
www.parks.ny.gov/golf-courses

HORSEBACK RIDING, BEACH & TRAIL RIDES

Deep Hollow Ranch Beach & Trail Rides
120 East Lake Drive - Montauk
631-668-2744
www.deephollowranch.com

Rita's Stables
Montauk Hwy - Montauk
631-668-5453

MINIATURE GOLF

Animal Kingdom Mini Golf
668 County Rd 39 – Southampton
631-283-2158

CMEE Mini Golf
376 Bridgehampton/Sag Harbor Turnpike – Bridgehampton
631-537-8250

Puff n' Putt
659 Montauk Hwy – Montauk
631-668-4473
Shelter Island Whales Tail
3 Ram Head Rd – Shelter Island
631-749-9601

PADDLE BOARDING

Global Boarding Water Sports
50 W. Water Street - Sag Harbor
631-537-8601
www.globalboarding.com

Main Beach Surf & Sport
352 Montauk Hwy - Wainscott
631-537-2716
www.mainbeach.com

Paddle Diva
219 Three Mile Harbor Hog Creek Road - East Hampton
631-329-2999
www.paddlediva.com

Peconic Water Sports
3253 Noyac Road - Sag Harbor
631-680-0111
www.peconicwatersports.com

Weekend Warrior Tours
8 Main Street - Sag Harbor
631-725-5950
www.weekendwarriortours.com

PUBLIC TENNIS COURTS

Abrahams Path Park
216 Abrahams Path – Amagansett
631-324-2417

Bridgehampton High School
2685 Montauk Hwy – Bridgehampton
631-537-0271

East Hampton High School
2 Long Lane – East Hampton
631-329-4143

Herrick Park
Park Place – East Hampton
631-329-4143

Montauk Downs State Park
50 S. Fairview Drive – Montauk
631-668-6264

Mashashimuet Park
Main Street – Sag Harbor
631-725-4018

Southampton High School
Leland Lane – Southampton
631-591-4600

Springs Recreation Area
Old Stone Hwy – Springs
631-324-2417

WATER SPORTS

BOAT RENTALS

Main Beach Surf & Sport
27 Montauk Hwy - Wainscott
631-537-2716
www.mainbeach.com

Sag Harbor Sailing, Inc
51 Pine Neck Avenue - Noyac
631 725-5100
www.sailsagharbor.com

Spring's General Store
29 Old Stone Hwy - East Hampton
631-329-5065
www.springsgeneralstore.com

Strong's Marine
1810 North Sea Road – Southampton
631-283-4841
www.strongsmarine.com

Uihlein's Marina & Boat Rental
444 West Lake Drive Ext - Montauk
631-668-3799
www.uihleinsmarina.com

VWeekend Warrior Tours
249 Main Street - Amagansett
631-267-2274
www.weekendwarriortours.com

BOAT CHARTERS

American Beauty Cruises
1 Bay Street - Sag Harbor
631-725-5211
www.americanbeautycruises.com

153

Blue Water Yacht Charters
Bay Street - Sag Harbor
631-725-4222

Hamptons Boat Rental
51 Division Street – Sag Harbor
800-417-2027
www.hamptonsboatrental.com

Mary Lloyd Charters
Boat Yard Lane – East Hampton
631-377-1780
www.marylloydcharters.com

Sag Harbor Charters
23 Marine Park Drive – Sag Harbor
631-456-1823
www.sagharborcharters.com

Sag Harbor Excursions
1 Long Wharf - Sag Harbor
631-599-3907
www.sagharborexcursions.com

Sag Harbor Sailing, Inc
51 Pine Neck Avenue - Noyac
631 725-5100
www.sailsagharbor.com

True East Charters
210 West Neck Road – Southampton
631-432-0900
www.trueeastcharters.com

FISHING CHARTERS

Capt Bob Sullivan Flyfishing & Light Tackle
Noyac - Montauk
631987-4402
www.sailsagharbor.com

Four C's Montauk Sportfishing
467 E. Lake Drive – Montauk
516-639-6767
www.fourcsfishingmontauk.com

Lazy Bones
474 West Lake Drive – Montauk
631-668-5671
www.montauksportfishing.com/lazybones

Montauk Fishing Charters
Montauk
631-668-1635
www.montaukfishingcharters.com

Dixon's To the Point Charters Flyfishing & Light Tackle
East Hampton & Montauk
516-314-1185
www.flyfishingmontauk.com

Blue Fin IV
59 Star Island Rd. – Montauk
631-668-9323
www.bluefiniv.com

Sea Wife IV
458 W. Lake Dr. – Montauk
844-282-7594
www.seawife.com

Oh Brother Montauk Charters
474 W. Lake Dr. – Montauk
631-668-2707

PARTY BOATS

Fin Chaser
59 Star Island Rd, - Montauk
516-643-0940
www.myfinchaser.com

Lazy bones
474 W. Lake Drive – Montauk
631-668-4671
www.montauksportfishing.com/lazybones

Mischell II
352 W. Lake Drive – Montauk
631-466-0694
www.mishell2fishingcharters.com

Miss Montauk
426 W. Lake Drive - Montauk
631-668-1545
www.missmontauk.com

Viking Fishing Fleet
462 W. Lake Drive – Montauk
631-668-5700
www.vikingfleet.com

SAILING

Montauk Sailing Charters & Sailing School
32 Star Island Rd – Montauk
631-522-5183
www.sailmontauk.com

Sag Harbor Sailing
51 Pine Neck, - Sag Harbor
631-725-5100
www.sailsagharbor.com

Sailing Montauks Catamaran Mon Tiki
32 Star Island Rd – Montauk
631-668-2826
www.sailingmontauk.com

Starlight Sailing Charters
1 Bay Street – Sag Harbor
917-388-0686
www.sailstarlight.com

Sailcat
27 Bay Street – Sag Harbor
631-682-8288
www.sailcat.com

SURF CASTING

Long Island Surf Fishing
Bill Wetzel
631-987-6919
www.longislandsurffishing.com

SCUBA DIVING

Hampton Dive Center
369 Flanders Rd - Riverhead
631-227-7578
www.hamptondive.com

SURFING

Air & Speed Surf Shop
795 Montauk Hwy - Montauk
631-668-0356
www.airandspeedclothing.com

Aloha Surf School
Surfing and Kiteboards
Ditch Plains - Montauk
631-377-6808
www.aloha-surfschool.com

CoreysWave Professional Surf Instruction
Montauk
516-639-4879
www.coreyswave.com

East End Surf Adventures
32 Windward - East Hampton
631-375-4106
www.eastendsurf.com

Flying Point Surfing School
516-885-6607
www.flyingpointsurfschool.com

Global Boarding
East Hampton – Montauk
631-537-8601
www.globalboarding.com

Hampton Surf Co.
Southampton - Montauk
631-495-1162
www.hamptonssurf.co

Hamptons Water Sports
1688 County Rd 39 - Southampton
631-283-9463
www.hamptonwatersports.com

Main Beach Surf & Sport
352 Montauk Hwy - Wainscott
631-537-2716
www.mainbeach.com

KITEBOARDING

Peconic Water Sports
Windsurfing, Kiteboarding, jet ski
64150 Main Street - Sag Harbor
631-680-0111
www.peconicwatersports.com

Skywalk Kiteboarding
Lessons and rentals
117 Main Street - East Hampton
631-324-4450
www.skywalkkiteboarding.com

Surfluca
Water Mill – Westhampton
www.surfluca.com

notes...

WINERIES AND VINEYARDS OF THE HAMPTONS

One Woman Vineyards

Sparkling Pointe

Jamesport Vineyards
The Wine Dock
The Old Field Vineyards
Mattabella Vineyards

Channing Daughters

Wolffer Estates

Duck Walk North
Anthony Napa Wines
The Winemaker Studio

Corey Creek Vineyards
Croteaux Vineyards
Onabay Vineyards
Sannino Bella Vita Vineyards
Raphael
Pindar Vineyards
Reilly Cellars

Duck Walk

Lieb Cellars

Puglese Vineyards

Peconic Bay Winery
Macari Vineyards

Waters Crest Winery

Castello di Borghese
Vineyards & Winery

McCall Vineyards
Pellegrini Vineyards
Roanoke Vineyards

Sherwood House Vineyards
Shinn Estate Vineyards

Gramercy Vineyards
Laurel Lake Vineyards
Clovis Point
Jason's Vineyards
Dilberto Winery
Sherwood House Vineyards
Jamesport Vineyards
Comtesse Therese Winery & Bistro

Suhru Wines and T'Jara Vineyards

Lieb Cellars
Sacarola Vineyards
Macari Vineyards & Winery
Harbes Family Vineyard

Suhru Wines and T'Jara Vineyards

Martha Clara Vineyards
Palmer Vineyards

Roanaoke Vineyard

Baiting Hollow Vineyard

VINEYARDS & WINERIES

SOUTH FORK

Channing Daughters Winery
1927 Scuttle Hole Road - **Bridgehampto**n
631-537-7224
www.channingdaughters.com

Duck Walk Vineyards
231 Montauk Highway - **Water Mill**
631-726-7555
www.duckwalk.com

Wolffer
 Estate Winery
139 Sagg Road - **Sagaponack**
www.wolffer.com

NORTH FORK

Anthony Nappa Wines
2885 Peconic Lane **– Peconic**
774-641-7488
www.anthonynappawines.com

Baiting Hollow Farm Vineyard
2114 Sound Ave **– Calverton**
631-369-0100
www.baitinghollowfarmvineyard.com

Bedell
36225 Main Road **- Cutchogue**
631-734-7537
www.bedellcellars.com

Castello Di Borghese
17150 County Road 48 - **Cutchogue**
631-734-5111
www.castellodiborghese.com

161

Clovis Point Wines
1935 Main Road -**Jamesport**
631-722-4222
www.clovispointwines.cm

Comtesse Therese Winery & Bistro
739 Main Street - **Aquebogue**
631-779-2800

Corey Creek Vineyards
45470 Route 25 - **Southold**
631-765-4168
www.bedellcellars.com

Croteaux
1450 S. Harbor Rd - **Southold**
631-765-6099
www.croteaux.com

Diliberto Winery
250 Manor Lane **– Jamesport**
631-722-3416
www.dilibertowinery.com

Duck Walk Vineyards North
44535 Main Street **– Southold**
631-765-3500
www.duckwalk.com

Harbes Family Vineyard
715 Sound Ave **– Mattituck**
631-298-WINE
www.harbesfamilyfarm.com

Jamesport Vineyards
1216 Main Road - **Jamesport**
631-722-5256
www.jamesportwines.com

Jason's Vineyard
1785 Main Road **– Jamesport**
631-238-5801
www.jasonsvineyard.com

Laurel Lake Vineyards
3165 Main St - **Laurel**
631-298-1420
www.llwines.com

Lenz
38355 NY Rt. 25 - **Peconic**
631-734-6010
www.lenzwine.com

Lieb
35 Cox Neck Rd - **Mattituck**
631-537-0025
www.liebcellars.com

Macari Vineyards & Winery
150 Bergen Ave. - **Mattituck**
631-289-0100
www.macariwines.com

Martha Clara Vineyards
2025 Sound Ave – **Riverhead**
631-298-0075
www.marthaclaravineyards.com

Mattebella Vineyards
46005 Route 25 – **Southold**
631-655-9554
www.mattebella.com

McCall Wines
22600 Route 25 – **Cutchogue**
631-734-5764
www.mccallwines.com

The Old Field Vineyards
59600 Main Road – **Southold**
631-765-0004
www.theoldfield.com

One Woman Wines & Vineyards
5195 Old North Road – **Southold**
631-765-1200
www.onewomanwines.com

Osprey's Dominion Vineyards
44075 Main Road - **Peconic**
631-765-6188
www.ospreysdominion.com

Palmer Vineyards
5120 Sound Ave. - **Riverhead**
631-722-9463
www.palmervineyards.com

Peconic Bay Winery
31320 Main Road - **Cutchogue**
631-734-7361
www.peconicbaywinery.com

Pellegrini Vineyards
23005 Main Road - **Cutchogue**
631-734-4111
www.pellegrinivineyards.com

Pindar Vineyards
37645 NY Rt. 25 - **Peconic**
631-734-6200
www.pindar.net

Pugliese Vineyards
34515 Main Road - **Cutchogue**
631-734-4057
www.pugliesevineyards.com

Raphael
39390 Route 25 – Peconic
631-765-1100
www.raphaelwine.com

Reilly Cellars
37025 Main Road – **Cutchogue**
516-446-2902
www.reillycellars.com

Roanoke Vineyards
165 Love Lane – **Mattituck**
631-298-7677
www.roanokevineyards.net

Sannino Vineyard
1375 Peconic Lane – **Peconic**
631-734 -8282
www.sanninovineyard.com

Sherwood House Vineyards
1291 Main Street – **Jamespor**t
631-779-2817
www.sherwoodhousevineyards.com

Scarola Vineyards
4850 Sound Ave - **Mattituck**
631-298-7676
www.scarolavineyards.com

Shinn Estate Vineyards
2000 Oregon Road – **Mattituck**
631-804-0367
www.shinnestatevineyards.com

Sparkling Pointe
3975 County Road 48- **Southold**
631-765-0200
www.sparklingpointe.com

Suhru Wines
35 Cox Neck Road – **Mattituck**
631-603-8127
www.suhruwinesny.com

Afterwards....

THE RULES

So the good news is, if you're reading this, you will be spending time in the Hamptons. It's the land of the rich and famous with miles of world renowned sandy beaches, over the top summer parties and endless outdoor activities . But, unless you are one the lucky few who live in paradise, your stay is only for so long. Make the best of it by using The Hamptons Lifesaver to guide you. It offers the low-down on where to drop the dry cleaning, buy bagels, or take the kiddos sailing...everything you need to have a blast in the Hamptons as if you had lived there for years.

There are a few rules that us locals would like to share to help you to enjoy, NO, survive the Hamptons like an old hand. Who wants to look like a tourist? These rules simply prevent the embarrassment of getting called out as a tourist (was going to put in another word here-rhymes with bass hole – but was overruled), or even worse, a day-tripper. So not cool!

RULE #1:

Don't go anywhere near the villages on a weekend. Smart visitors and locals do all their shopping midweek. They shop at the farm stands and local fish markets. They buy local.

RULE #2:

Do not lease, rent or visit in an SUV the size of Rhode Island just because it's cool, roomy and sporty...and you can carry all your friends. If you do, you will be sorry, especially when you break RULE #1 (which everybody does) and head into the village on a weekend rationalizing Oh it can't be that bad. It will make your

167

experience even worse...besides the fact that there will be no spaces no matter how many times you enjoy the gridlock circling the village...when that miracle does finally happen...and the great sea of cars opens and gives you a spot, there is no doubt that the cozy little space will be sandwiched between an equally oversized SUV politely sharing a good foot of your spot and a car so over-priced that the driver does not have to obey the parking lines. At this point, you will dread having to give up that spot to the smug little Prius driver patiently blaring his horn behind you as you sob over having to pass up THE SPOT. Walk, bike, keep it small... you will thank me for this one. Let your friends figure out their own transportation. They are probably using you for your rental anyway.

RULE #3:

Do not use your cell phone in public. It's annoying and no one wants to hear you shout about your plans for the next 24 hours over the person next to you who is shouting about their latest medical procedure over the person next to them babbling on about their latest lawsuit or real estate victory. None of us want to hear it. No-one cares!

RULE #4:

Do not threaten to sue the maître d' for failing to seat you for breakfast as promptly as you'd like. No one cares how big and powerful you are. Everyone in the Hamptons gets to wait in the same line when they break RULE #1, including lawyers(though some are thinking about banning them from the Hamptons alto-gether). If you are a lawyer disregard this last comment.

RULE #5:

While it is ok to dress like a slob, it is not ok to act like a slob. I think this one is self-explanatory. If not, maybe the Hamptons isn't the spot for you?

RULE #6:

It is ok to wave at fellow drivers (even smile). It is not ok to hold up one's hand to confirm that you have come up with your own traffic pattern and that all other drivers should let you follow this route unimpeded...Also, horns are not required in the Hamptons, please don't use them like you are in the city.

RULE #7:

Bring a book, or books...

RULE #8:

If going out to any one of the siren restaurants (they are sooo good you will break RULE #1), plan ahead...If the place is worth a damn, it will be crowded especially in the height of the season. Call ahead and make a reservation. And be nice to the staff. ALSO, please refer to RULE #3...It still stands, no one wants to hear about your open heart surgery while eating their steak. In addition, while at dinner try to talk to only those at your table... not the entire restaurant. No one else cares about your upcoming movie deal that exists only in your imagination.

RULE #9:

Go outside and do something. Go paddle boarding, go fishing, go lay on a beach...just go out and do stuff because at the end of the day that is what the Hamptons is about. And you cannot appreciate those world class beaches if you're inside.

RULE #10:

Get to the beach early and stay there. They really are the best in the world. If the weather is nice and you aren't there, you are missing the point of the summer in the Hamptons (and because again parking can be horrendous).

So remember take a breath and relax...OK maybe the rent for your little foray to summer paradise was a tad steep (like so steep that you need to convince your eldest child that maybe college isn't the way to go) but there is nothing you can do about that now. Don't be one of the mindless zombies stressing as they try to fit every possible activity into a 48-hour window before the return trip to life on Monday. And while there is a cool charity fundraiser for a great cause held almost every second of the day during the season, pick the causes that matter to you and don't try to hit them all. It's impossible and you will never be able to afford the rental next year.

My best advice, pick a few activities, plan ahead and you'll make the memories that have been keeping people coming to the Hamptons for over 100 years.

Oh and one more thing, I am a firm believer that rules are made to be broken, especially when on vacation, but not RULE #3. I still don't want to listen to your latest dating disasters (although to be honest, sometimes those are the only good calls). I want to listen to the waves and the seagulls. Have a great summer in paradise.

Paddy South

acknowledgements...

A heartfelt thanks to everyone who has contributed via text and email throughout this past year keeping me updated with new shops, services and restaurants. I'm touched you care so much about our beautiful beach community - the east end.

Thank you to my dad, Charles Holmes, for being my editor and my sound board and for being so supportive of everything I do. I love you.

Thank you to Jessie Gauger. You rock as a fact checker and you make a mean Swedish meatball sister!

Many thanks to my cool brother in law Paddy South who wrote the After-word "10 Rules" of the Hamptons. I had to include them again this year. Your sense of humor never fails to entertain me.

Alejandra Murillo you are so amazing. I can't believe you walked into my life at the 9th hour! You got me and what I was looking for with illustra-tions right from the start. You are so talented. I can't wait to hang a piece of your art on my wall.

And most of all a huge thank you to Bob Sullivan for muddling through this entire process with me. You kept me on track, so I could meet the deadline. We did it! I absolutely could not have done this without you!!

Tracey Holmes has been a long time resident of the Hamptons and has a passion for all the many unique and wonderful qualities that make the area so special. She embraces her work as a real estate professional with the Corcoran Group and in her spare time enjoys all the special aspects of living on the beautiful East End.

Made in the USA
Columbia, SC
30 July 2018